THE F

of Humanity and the Earth

THE FUTURE
of Humanity and the Earth

as foreseen by
RUDOLF STEINER

RICHARD SEDDON

TEMPLE LODGE

Temple Lodge Publishing
Hillside House, The Square
Forest Row, East Sussex
RH18 5ES

www.templelodge.com

Published by Temple Lodge 2002

A catalogue record for this book is available from the British Library

ISBN 1 902636 29 5

Cover picture: *Slavic Man* by Rudolf Steiner
Cover layout by S. Gulbekian
Typeset by DP Photosetting, Aylesbury, Bucks.
Printed and bound by Cromwell Press Limited, Trowbridge, Wilts.

He who does not know how to take account of
three thousand years remains in the dark without
experience. Let him live from day to day.

Goethe – Westöstlicher Divan – 1819

The future slumbers in human beings, and needs
only to be awakened. It cannot be created.

Paul Klee – 1901

May the future rest on the past,
The past come to feel the future
For vigorous present existence.
May in inner resilience of life
World-being wakefulness gain power,
Life's strength for action come to flower.
May the past bear the future.

Rudolf Steiner
Verse for Capricorn

Contents

Preface

In seeking to understand the process of evolution, modern civilization stands like a schizophrenic between two opposing viewpoints. On the one hand are ancient descriptions of a magical creation by an omnipotent yet unknowable God. On the other is the modern materialistic theory of an equally inexplicable 'big bang', from which the enormous subtlety of the universe and of human life is supposed to follow by necessity. Arguments are adduced to support both views, and both are open to question. As is common in such situations, the truth is likely to lie between them, in which the insights of spiritual life (but not necessarily the dogmas) are brought together with the phenomena (but not necessarily the theories) of scientific observation.

Such a third viewpoint existed in ancient times within the secrecy of the mysteries, and hints of it were given in the form of myths, sagas and texts. It was expressed more specifically, but still in imaginative pictures, in the Apocalypse of St John, which contains a great part of esoteric Christianity. It describes a path both of self-development (initiation) for the priest and of the development of the whole of humanity for long ages to come. This is very hard for the ordinary consciousness of today to understand, or even to recognize. But in modern times both aspects have been set out in clear concepts by Rudolf Steiner (1861–1925). This outlook is guided by the words of Christ: 'I have many things to say to you, but you cannot bear them now … When the Spirit of Truth comes … he will declare to you the things that are to come' (John 16: 12). Moreover reincarnation enables every human being to participate in this future.

In his book *An Outline of Occult Science* (1910),* Rudolf Steiner laid the foundation for the view here presented, without a grasp of which much of it must appear speculative. He shows that the all-essential causes of what happens on earth do not lie in outer nature, which proceeds according to already existing laws; they lie in the deeds of creative spiritual beings who work through mankind and may be known on the inward path. He therefore starts from an analysis of the full spiritual, soul and bodily nature of the human being, of which a very brief sketch is given in Appendix 1. Then, based on his own spiritual research, he gives a tremendous picture of the work of the divine Hierarchies in the course of evolution, through which human beings (and at the same time the kingdoms of nature) were brought into existence. Humanity is central to this view, rather than peripheral as it is for academic science, and this is of the greatest significance; for what is said derives from human experience extended in the way described, not from either hypothesis or dogma.

The present study is an elaboration of Chapter 6 of Steiner's book, based on some 300 of his lectures, especially the cycle *The Apocalypse of St John*. But it concerns only one aspect of the Apocalypse, which has quite other dimensions,† and is not a commentary on it. The consistency of these lectures, given over 20 years, is quite remarkable. The content which follows is based directly on Steiner's words, but the placing of references to 'the future' necessarily depends on the editor. In particular, he gave no known indications of when either the planets or the layers within the earth are to be reabsorbed into the spirit, and guidance has here been sought from correspondences with the Apocalypse of St John.

---

*Republished as *An Outline of Esoteric Science*, New York, 1998.
† See: Rudolf Steiner, *The Book of Revelation and the Work of the Priest*, London, 1998.

Understanding of this view depends on insight into the cosmic rhythms of time, and these are first established by reference to past ages. The future development of individuals within these rhythms lies in the path of self-knowledge which forms the core of Steiner's work, but since this needs to be accurately understood no attempt is made to summarize it here.*

Only notes exist of lectures prior to 1908, written up afterwards by earnest esoteric students, so turns of phrase cannot be relied on as verbatim; and Steiner had no opportunity to verify stenographic reports. The oriental terminology he used to suit his early audiences is replaced here by that which he later evolved for the West, and consistency has been given to words such as 'epoch' used variously by translators (and sometimes by Steiner himself). The word 'today' refers to our present time, the turn of the millennium, whereas 'now' refers in the dramatic present to the period under consideration. The attempt is made to mould available details into an accessible narrative; but cognate remarks by Steiner are incorporated for contemplation even if they do not read smoothly, rather than omit them.

Just as a seed dissected for examination under the microscope will not subsequently bear fruit, so this description is not intended for intellectual dissection, but will only be fruitful if taken up as a whole into the imagination and meditatively digested. It can then be a powerful incentive for the individual will, a source of purpose, strength and courage. Yet it is no more than a husk, to be cast off as soon as one's own seedling experience of spiritual reality to which it points begins to unfold.

Without the support of my wife Mary, despite problems of health, and the help of other friends, this study could not

---

*See: *An Outline of Occult Science*, Chapter 5.

have been completed. May it stimulate others to deeper insight.

Richard Seddon
Easter 2001

1
Introduction

The Problem of Prediction

If meteorologists, for example, cannot with all their equipment accurately forecast the weather a week ahead, how can it be possible to say anything of value about the future of mankind and of the universe over millennia? If human beings can act in freedom, does this not make it even more impossible?

It must at once be admitted that with the ordinary faculties of modern consciousness, and with information drawn only from sense-perception (including its extension through physical instruments), there can be no such possibility. But there have always been exceptional individuals who through rigorous self-development have been able to unfold within themselves successively higher levels of consciousness that extend widely in time. In past ages such people were revered as the initiates of the mysteries, whether of East or West, or as prophets of the Old Testament. They spoke of long past events from inner experience, a spiritual remembering known as 'reading in the Akashic Record', and to some extent spoke also of the future.

Out of such a consciousness, coupled with his special destiny with Jesus Christ, St John was not only able to say, 'In the beginning was the Word ... all things were made by him,' but was also able to perceive in Christ's life those forces which carry forward what he made, and will metamorphose it in the future. He saw how the destiny lived through in the three years will gradually become the destiny of the whole of mankind.[1] That is why he could also write the Apocalypse, showing for Christian priest-initiates

in majestic pictures three further stages of evolution. After
the 'letters' referring to the present epoch, the seven 'seals'
depict a future at a first level ('come up hither and I will
show you what must happen hereafter' — Rev. 4: 1); the
seven 'trumpets' sound inspirations of a second level; then
'God's temple in heaven was laid open' (Rev. 11: 19),
leading to a third level that includes the emergence and
defeat of three 'beasts', and the descent of the New
Jerusalem.

Similarly St Paul speaks of a man (his higher self) who
was 'caught up to the third heaven' (2 Cor. 12: 2). He
founded a school of esoteric Christianity to cultivate this
'hidden wisdom of God' (1 Cor. 2: 7), carried on by
Dionysius the Areopagite (whose work on the Hierarchies
was disseminated only later). But the western church systematically destroyed such wisdom, because it was seen as
historically necessary that individuals should be freed from
knowledge of their divine origin, in order to come to it
afresh in freedom. Nevertheless this esoteric wisdom
flowed on secretly in such movements as Manichaeism and
its offshoots, in the Knights Templar, in the Rosicrucian
brotherhood and elsewhere.

At the turn of the twentieth century Rudolf Steiner
developed such capacities, in modern form, to a high
degree (and outlined his method in his book *Knowledge of the
Higher Worlds*). He described in his book *Theosophy* these
same three worlds in detail, naming them the soul world,
and Lower and Higher Spiritland respectively. Though
distinct for human consciousness, they are of course totally
integrated in the one reality. In lectures he explained how,
just as we have an idea what to do, feel enthusiasm for it,
picture the best way to do it, and then act, so do the Hierarchies when preparing the future. Their impulses arise as
thought-germs in Higher Spiritland, become more specific
in Lower Spiritland, are shaped into images in the soul

world, and finally become physical reality.[2] In the soul world time operates in reverse, in the sense that the result is seen before the cause. So there it is as natural to see the astral future as it is here to see the physical past. In such circumstances prophetic vision is possible. Moreover in all aspects, great and small, the forces active in building up a situation (even a planet) must be taken into account in its respiritualization — that is karma.

Thus an initiate who can see and also think at these higher levels can grasp what is in active preparation for future humanity. Through his initiation he experiences in advance the path which humanity will tread in ages to come. This is neither a dogmatic nor an inferential but an experiential understanding, which concerns the general laws of future evolution but does not preclude individual freedom to act within those laws.

Such insight into what is growing and becoming cannot of course be grasped by narrow conceptions that seek for proof. Those are suited only to what belongs to the past and is already set; the future must be grasped by effort and activity of the soul, which adapts itself to the changes which it seeks to understand. Moreover insight is here not a mere matter of knowledge, for the thoughts of spiritual research become real, practical ideals which actually confer a future on the earth. Such knowlege is worthless if it is not changed into deeds, into living impulses of feeling, and into certainty in life. To set aims in this way means in the highest sense to grasp Christianity esoterically — this is how the author of the Apocalypse understood it.[3]

The Pattern of Evolution

Everyone knows from direct experience the difference between eating, drinking, breathing and warming up, and between the corresponding modes of voidance; they relate to the discrete states of the solid, fluid, air and warmth respectively. Everyone also knows the difference between minerals, plants, animals and humans (who alone can walk upright, speak and think). And everyone can distinguish between being awake, dreaming, sleeping deeply and a state of trance or coma. These simple, common-sense observations indicate that evolution has not been a continuous process, but one that alternates rhythmically between four phases of manifestation and inwardization, just as at a mundane level we alternate between waking and sleeping. This was clearly recognized in the ancient mysteries as a process involving the whole solar system, and the four steps were named Saturn, Sun, Moon and Earth respectively.

Rudolf Steiner described in detail in his book *An Outline of Occult Science* how the successive stages were brought about by the deeds of the spiritual Hierarchies; and meditative study of the pictures he presented is an essential preliminary to any modern insight into the processes concerned, of which only a bare hint is possible here. Evolution is found to proceed in various 'layers' of time, somewhat comparable to the layers found in the chaos phenomena of space. Each layer is sevenfold, which is as much inherent in the inner experience of time as three dimensions are inherent in the ordinary experience of space. Nevertheless the first and last stages are really transitional, so that only five show significant progress. The primary significance of evolution is found to consist in the fact that beings belonging to all ranks of the Hierarchies, of which mankind is today but the lowest, progress at each stage to a higher *condition of consciousness*, and thus pass from receivers to givers.

Real knowlege can only reach back to a time when some element of the human being existed. This is the Saturn condition, when a loving, courageous sacrifice of their substance by exalted, already existing beings known as the Thrones or Spirits of Will engendered a warmth of soul, which later manifested in outer living warmth. This warmth was shaped from the zodiac by the Cosmic Word (the shaping force of sound is well known) into primitive bodies of mere warmth, precursors of our physical bodies ('In the beginning was the Word' — John 1: 1). From the spiritual substance of this sacrifice Time Beings (Archai) acquired their ego, and time itself began (hence it is unreal to ask what was 'before' Saturn). The bodies were then worked on by the Archai, and briefly acquired a consciousness equivalent to coma, a pure wonderment, before dissolving.

During the Sun condition the Spirits of Wisdom bestowed their life-substance, the origin of our etheric* bodies, and the Archangels acquired their ego. After a time they reflected back part of the bestowal in such a way that it glowed with light, the outstreaming and return creating a two-dimensional space. Part of the warmth was condensed to transient bodies of air endowed with life, which had a sleeping consciousness equivalent to the way in which plants today react to light.

During the Moon condition, through the gift of the Spirits of Motion of their astral* substance from which our astral body originated, chemical processes developed, and part of the bodies condensed further to a fluid in various conditions of congealment in three dimensions. These bodies acquired a dreamlike picture-consciousness comparable to that of the higher animals today. This was furthered by the work of the Angels, who were then acquiring their ego (though not all achieved their goal). The Moon condition is the source

---

*For the meaning of these terms please see Appendix 1.

of all the wisdom built into the kingdoms of nature today.

Only at the fourth stage did consolidation reach the formation of a solid earth, when the Spirits of Form (Elohim, Exusiai) sacrificed their ego-substance to enable mankind itself to develop the waking ego-consciousness that we have today. This process is considered further below. Three further stages will be described in Chapter 9, named the Jupiter, Venus and Vulcan conditions, during which humanity is to perfect three higher levels of consciousness. These seven conditions of consciousness are called in the Apocalypse 'the seven stars' (Rev. 1: 15).

The evolution of the Earth condition itself takes place in seven *Conditions of Life*, beginning with three which recapitulated the stages of Saturn, Sun and Moon in a complex manner. We exist now in the fourth, mineral Condition of Life, so called not only because there is for the first time a solid mineral foundation, but because the specific mineral quality of separation in space enables our thinking to grasp the concept of separation, and thus of a separate human ego independent from its divine origin. (In the other Conditions of Life, to be described in Chapter 8, states of continuous metamorphosis prevail.)

Everything in each Condition of Life passes through seven *stages of form* (Chapter 7). These progress, as already mentioned on pages 6–7, from Higher to Lower Spiritland (where there is neither space nor time), thence to the soul world (which exists in time but not space), and finally to physical-etheric manifestation in time and space. It is all subsequently carried back in altered state through the soul world to Lower and Higher Spiritland. These seven stages are together present around us as past, present and future, and comprise the total sphere of reality.

Even the physical form of the mineral Condition of Life on the earth has evolved through seven *epochs*, which again first echo Saturn, Sun and Moon (Chapter 5). Thus the earliest, known as the Polarean, consisted of fiery warmth, later compressed at the centre of the earth, and human bodies consisted only of fine etheric warmth. The second epoch, the Hyperborean, saw the separation of the sun and moon-earth, enabling human bodies on the latter to condense to a gaseous condition whilst the sun beings could progress without hindrance. During the third epoch, the Lemurian, bodies on the moon-earth densified still further to the point where the proto-human astral beings could no longer use them, and most were drawn away to other planets by luciferic spirits. A very few survived on earth whilst the moon was withdrawn by Jehovah together with the densest forces, thus providing bodies to which the others could gradually return. That was when the events described in Genesis 2 and 3 occurred — the breathing of the living soul into these bodies of warmth and air within a still fluid atmosphere, and everything connected with the Fall. Now there evolved more solid substance, which hardened later during the geological period when primal forms of animal and plant became incorporated.

Only with the fourth, central epoch known as Atlantis can one speak of human races, but these were at first still soft and animal-like, without a solid skeleton (hence the 'missing link'), though they did have a living companionship with beings of the spiritual world. Meanwhile the reptiles of the Jurassic and the mammals of the Cainozoic trod the still living, malleable earth. Only later came the premature hardening of the first hominids. Finally, modern human forms evolved during the Ice Ages and the settling of the continents into their present pattern, leaving hardened skeletons. After consideration of the present epoch, the future sixth and seventh epochs will be described in Chapters 5 and 6.

Although every epoch also proceeds in seven stages, it is

only in our fifth (Post-Atlantean) epoch that one can first speak of *cultural ages*, each guided by a different Archon as Spirit of the Age. We shall distinguish in the next section the ancient Indian, Persian, Egypto-Chaldean, Graeco-Roman and our own, with a sixth and seventh to be described in Chapters 3 and 4. Each of these is first prepared and then influenced by forces from one particular constellation. For example, the vernal point (where the sun rises on 21 March) stands in Pisces from AD 215 to 2965 and this influences our present age which extends from 1415 to 3575. Even so, impulses from a previous age continue for a long time before they are transformed by those of the new.

Even within a cultural age, humanity is guided for shorter periods of about 350 years by one of seven successive *Archangels of Time* (pp. 26–40), who bear impulses from the 'traditional' planets in a sequence which counterbalances that of planetary evolution. These are known as Michael, Oriphiel, Aniel, Zachariel, Raphael, Samael and Gabriel. Their influences also take time to become effective, and may predominate for a century or more during the next rulership.* Still shorter rhythms can also be traced, especially the 33-year rhythm of the life of Jesus Christ.

This brief outline of the layers of time is expressed diagramatically in Appendix 2, but must be regarded only as explanatory. Irregularities begin as mankind extricates itself from the rigidification of the past.

The Post-Atlantean Epoch

This epoch needs to be sketched more fully before we proceed to the future, because what humanity has already

---

*The working of these Archangels since ancient Greece is studied in the author's *Europa – A Spiritual Biography*.

experienced has not passed entirely into oblivion. Traces remain unconsciously within us, and will reappear in future so that we may work them over and transform them through the power of Christ.

First came the original pre-Vedic culture of India (late eighth to sixth millennium BC). Consciousness was then dominated by the loss of the full Atlantean clairvoyance of the spiritual world ('You have left your first love' — Rev. 2: 4). But neither did people yet see the outer world through the senses as we do; they regarded the sense-impressions as *maya*, illusion, and hated them (Rev. 2: 6). They were, however, still enveloped in an etheric aura which they beheld inwardly, and like young children beheld in en-souled pictures the thoughts inspired within them by the gods. They sensed directly the sympathy and antipathy of one another, and were able to heal through the power of the word. They thus felt a certain unity between the inner and outer worlds, expressed in the words 'I am that'. All this was prepared from the constellation of Cancer, the Crab, which encloses an inner nature within the protective shell of the chest. Only through initiation was it possible to rise above the caste into which one was born as a result of previous karma. Initiates made the etheric body a bearer of memory by means of yoga, and thus prepared the warmth of the blood to receive the ego; thereby what the Polarean epoch lived through became for them knowledge. Only the Seven Holy Rishis, inspired by Archai, were still able to speak of the Atlantean wisdom, and of the Godhead as Brahman, the All One, into whom they wished to be reabsorbed.

The second cultural age was that of ancient Persia or Iran (fifth and fourth millennia BC). The eternal sun forces were now experienced in sleep as a realm of light filled with the working of Christ, named by Zarathustra and his pupils as Ahura Mazda; whilst earthly reality experienced by day, called the kingdom of Ahriman, was a realm of comparative darkness. Yet it was felt as a copy of the divine, and as such they felt it their task to transform and respiritualize it by means of work—hence the beginning of agriculture. This duality was prepared from the constellation of Gemini, the Twins; and it expressed in conceptual form (inspired by Archangelic beings) what the Hyperboreans had experienced as the actual separation of sun and earth. The polarity of light and dark was at the same time experienced as a polarity of good and evil. As they worked in the sense world, consciousness entered the sentient body.* On the inner path, which no longer coincided with the outer, people perceived the astral body* instead of the spirit, and met there the forces of Lucifer (later called Mithras).

The third age, the Egypto-Chaldean (2900–747 BC) includes the Assyrian, Babylonian, Semitic and Hibernian cultures. Consciousness, now feeling sheltered within the bloodstream, permeated the sentient soul,* which directed it outwards, imbuing sensations arising from the spirit in nature with living thoughts received from the Angels. Under the influence of the Bull this age consequently penetrated fully into this external world, and learned to treasure the physical plane (hence, for example, the practice of mummification). They lovingly deciphered the cosmic writing of the visible stars—still known as dwellings of divine beings—and then applied their insights, like inspired teenagers, to practical affairs, predetermining matters of state, measuring the earth and the heavens, weighing and calculating. Their mystery wisdom expressed experiences of the Lemurian epoch. For example, the trinity of sun, moon and earth then separated was pictured in Osiris, Isis and Horus; loss of vision of the soul world in the death of Osiris; experience of separate sense-data in his dismemberment; pre-human bodies in their animal-headed

---

*For the meaning of these terms please see Appendix 1.

deities. An actual incarnation of Lucifer, the tempter who gave man knowledge of good and evil at the Fall, occurred in China during the third millennium BC.[4] From him flowed much of the subsequent wisdom of the East and of the Greek age, but not moral impulses; for except in Judaism people still felt themselves members of the cosmos. The wisdom of Hermes/Thoth subsequently became corrupted, however, to black magic (Rev. 2: 14).

The fourth, Graeco-Roman age (747 BC–AD 1413) still echoed the Atlantean epoch, with its many divine etheric forms portrayed as gods in human image (in the Arthurian Mysteries, in purely human terms). The forces of Aries, the Ram, prepared the age to take in the universe, for example as geometry, and look back on it. The Greek sought to harmonize perfectly with his environment, developing an inner personal and intellectual culture through which to free the soul from the spiritual world, making fundamental mystery wisdom accessible to all by means of poetry, drama and sculpture, and through philosophy establishing the faculties of reasoned thought and feeling.

Into this came the descent of Christ into the specially prepared Hebrew people. Although mankind was unable to understand the significance of this — despite the efforts of Gnosticism to do so — the new impulse of love for one another extending beyond the family blood-bond was received. Through Christ the individual ego was finally born within the feeling mind of those who took up that impulse. 'I will reward each of you according to his deeds' (Rev. 2: 23).

But through Rome, with its emphasis on conquest and personality, came a darkening. The wisdom of the ancient mysteries was systematically suppressed. With the descent of the cosmic intelligence and the 'I' from the angelic world to the human intellectual soul about AD 333, thoughts became dead, and the search for understanding was replaced by dogma. In AD 869 the spirit as separate reality was formally denied by a council of the Roman Church. Meanwhile AD 666 designates the impulse of Arabism modified by Mohammedanism, which knows only the Father, and would do away for ever with all freedom, the gift of Christ. Death thus entered evolution in a new way, and confidence in the spirit was lost. The concept of Christendom became for most people (the scholastics excepted) little more than the ideal of universal brotherhood.

Nevertheless, as already mentioned, an esoteric Christianity—branded by the Church as heretical—remained active behind the scenes. 'Hold fast to what you have until I come' (Rev. 2: 25). Mani founded a religion devoted to transforming evil into good (rather than trying to exterminate it). The knights of the Grail nurtured an inner experience of Christ, which was developed by Parzival into a path of initiation for the consciousness soul.[5] The Rosicrucians brought the wisdom of pre-Christian ages to a single focus and applied it as a healing impulse. In such movements the words 'I am the bread of life' (John 6: 35) were sincerely experienced; for bread is created by the good sun forces in union with the earth, and is worked on by human beings for the nourishment of the bodies of others.

Thus during the fifteenth century our fifth age dawned with a thinking that was almost universally dead (i.e. applicable only to inorganic mineral conditions). Warmth of heart had little power in world affairs; mankind had become the slave of outer conditions of comfort, of matter. But inwardly a completely new age was waiting to struggle through the thicket of the establishment.

The Start of the Fifth Age

The fifth, Anglo-Germanic age began in 1413 and will extend until 3573. Although we might suppose that we understand it because we live in it, we have so far seen only its earliest stages. It has hitherto been dominated by the Anglo-Saxon people, whose task is to develop the consciousness soul—that element in us which is to be freed from all traces of sympathy and antipathy, of egoism, and is to carry an objectivity similar to that of mathematics into all spheres of life, especially the social, so that the truths of the spirit can be born into it. The awakening of this soul is still in its beginnings, and will require a metamorphosis of present society and its forms of life.

This is the first age that has no previous epoch to recapitulate, but has instead to develop out of itself something new that can lead into the future. It carries the future within it like a seed. At first, however, it spiritually looked backwards. Theology tied itself to ancient documents rather than developing the inner experiences to which they point. Science tied thinking down to the wrought work of the material world, instead of detecting the spirit in nature, as does Goetheanism. Social life is tied by the very structure of society to forms evolved in ancient Egypt, to the cult of personality evolved in Rome, and to the demands of egoism. We therefore experience progressive deterioration both in culture and in human relationships.

Samael, the Archangel of Mars, was nearing the end of his quarrelsome rule as Time Archangel when the age began. Under his aegis the universality of Christendom had been broken up by the intellectual attack of Nominalism, the physical attacks of the Mongols, the impulse of the Renaissance looking back to Rome and Greece, and a growing political awareness of nationhood. But in the free towns the consciousness soul began to awaken, for example in the guilds. It was at this time that the cosmic intelligence was carried from the heart to the head, the nerve-sense system; from being heart-centred, human beings became increasingly centred in their heads.[6]

Around 1471 spiritual rulership passed to Gabriel, the Archangel of the moon. His period was dominated by the rise of the nation-state and of natural science (both firmly rooted in the moon forces of heredity), and by the Reformation and Counter-Reformation.

Gabriel brought also the moon quality of occultism, which enabled the impulses of ancient Egypt, now out of due time, to work again in an adverse way. We find here the third age echoing in the fifth, pivoted around the Mystery of Golgotha, but not yet its true Christianization. The hierarchy of a society ruled by a Pharaoh underlies the modern hierarchies of industry, Church and state. Measure, number and weight are the only realities for science, which cannot handle qualitative values. Mummification—an undue valuing of the material—reappears in materialism. Osiris as sun-god reappears in the sun-centred conception of the universe—indeed Kepler said, 'I will carry the sacred ceremonial vessels of Egypt into the modern world.' And ancient rituals reappear in Freemasonry, which gained a specially powerful hold over money, and over a worldwide empire based on economics. The age of Pisces, bringing the impulse of the trader, has begun in a physical manner.

Behind the scenes, Gabriel, also the Angel of the Annunciation, was invisibly adapting the physical brain to enable a new and objective living thinking to be introduced in the next period. This already made possible at the beginning of the nineteenth century the flowering of German philosophy, which reached a correct understanding of the eternal cosmic 'I'; but this was overwhelmed. Instead democracy, socialism and bureaucracy, based on the lowest common factor of mundane egoism, rose with elemental force.

Meanwhile Michael, the Sun Archangel, who strides ahead of Christ as his countenance, was preparing a new spiritual content for humanity in a supersensible school in the spiritual world, attended by both human and super-human beings, during the fifteenth to early eighteenth centuries; and he transformed this content into a super-sensible ritual for his followers in the early nineteenth. His rulership of 350 years as Time Archangel began in 1879. But before that he was further elevated in 1841 to take over the role of Spirit of the Age for the whole period until 3573, the task of an Archon. He now therefore carries a dual responsibility, which is still in its early stages and has yet to attain its full power.

The Twentieth Century

In 1899, soon after Michael took up his dual role, Kali Yuga, the Dark Age of 5000 years, came to an end. The etheric body began the long process of separating again from the physical body, carrying mankind as a whole unknowingly across the threshold of the spiritual world. On the one hand, thinking, feeling and willing cease to be coordinated by the physical body, so that unless this is done consciously we find plans divorced from reality, acts devoid of feeling, growing uncertainty and anxiety. On the other hand, spiritual light again became visible on earth through Rudolf Steiner's anthroposophy or spiritual science, and a new cosmic impulse was thereby born. But the counter-forces took powerful hold of this situation, and it should be obvious that the mind-set that has enabled them to do so is inadequate to resolve the consequences.*

The essential fact is that we live unaware in the midst of a mighty spiritual battle for the future of humanity between

---

*Steiner's remarks on many aspects are outlined in the editor's booklet *The End of the Millennium and Beyond*.

Christ and the opposing powers, the scale of which we can hardly imagine. Most people have not even perceived that there are two different opponents: Lucifer, the tempter, who inspires egoism and would draw humanity back from life to the glories of the past; and Ahriman, Satan, the father of lies, who inspires the rat race, and would chain humanity for ever to the earth. Christ holds the balance, and we need to find with him the middle way.

Lucifer and Ahriman conspire today above all to eliminate all recognition of the human soul in all sorts of ways — for example, by describing brain-processes as the causes, rather than the effect, of soul-phenomena. The time when souls will be made effectively non-existent by means of a drug, preferably administered in infancy, is not far off. Thereby they seek to prevent any further spiritual development of mankind.

Furthermore, just as Lucifer once incarnated in the East in the third millennium BC, so before only a part of the third millennium AD has elapsed Ahriman will incarnate in a human being in the West. His preparations are already far advanced.[7] Due to Ahriman's inspiration we have a natural science — and with it the thinking of much of humanity — which recognizes only the animal within us, ignoring the human identity as spirit (which was denied by the Church a thousand years ago). We have already seen men with animal gestures in their faces and destructive fury in their emotions, who not only ridicule the spirit but thrust it down into the slough.

Under the influence of Lucifer and Ahriman a society has developed, the whole structure of which — whether in industry, education, sport or whatever — is based on selfishness, competition and rivalry, instead of on loving help to one another. That is left to caring individuals. The result has been two world wars, many smaller ones, and ethnic cleansing; totalitarianism, Bolshevism and the Holocaust;

drugs and violence; destruction of the ozone layer and tropical forests and wildlife. Much more could be added. The vice of the age is deceit, the karmic result of a super-ficial life. Western civilization is in fact the beginning of the earth's death, and will perish with it. 'He who has the seven spirits of God [Appendix 1] and the seven stars (p. 10) says: I know your deeds; you have the name of being alive, and are dead. Be alert! And establish what remains that is about to die' (Rev. 3: 2).

Only by individually suffering and confronting in free-dom this scenario of death is the consciousness soul to be developed. For death in all its forms must be recognized as the benefactor that enables us individually to rise above an existence that separates us from the spirit. Only through death can we reach the forces of resurrection. It is in fact a manifestation of the Father-principle, and the upward path begins with reverence for all that flows from the Father.

Whereas before, say, 1870 everything was made of nat-ural materials, and previously people had been aware of the elemental beings of nature, today we live amid the products of technology — plastic, concrete, steel, electronics etc. — from which the natural beings have been driven out by high pressure and temperatures, and replaced by beings con-trived by the human intellect, which are of an ahrimanic nature. We are in great danger of losing the forces of nature out of which we were created, and of sliding down into the ahrimanic world of sub-nature which we have made. Sci-ence has lost insight into the human being, and intellectual religion has denied the spirit in nature. Only through finding the forces of Christ in the etheric can we retain our humanity. Environmentalism expresses the longing for this. Knowledge of the spirit must re-enter everyday life.

It has to be admitted that the form in which Christianity has been presented for 2000 years has at best failed to permeate modern culture, and is no longer sufficient. But that does not mean that Christianity itself has failed! Unless mankind turns to the realities of the spirit, and to the self-disciplines of esoteric Christianity suited to today, things can only deteriorate further. More and more people need to overcome the spectre of old ideas, and to experience thinking as a spiritual activity. They must find the way from the weak everyday ego to an 'I' which experiences its cosmic stature; and replace sleepy instinctive reactions and fears by compassionate deeds performed alertly in freedom and love. On this the future of humanity depends; but just for this reason the opposing powers make every effort to prevent it.

Moreover certain brotherhoods of the West actively promulgate belief in materialism in order that such materialists shall remain in the earth sphere after they die, and become the means through which the brotherhoods can acquire a quite particular power over others for their own ends.

Christ is, however, in our age the cosmic and earthly Healer. As a cosmic being from outside the earth he brings healing forces to those who actively seek them. Mankind suffers under the fear of heredity, and is near to losing the spirit altogether. But spiritual science is the therapy that brings vigour and health. Moreover, since 1933 Christ has become visible to a small number of people as an etheric figure (p. 28), and this will increase. Through him a *completely new culture* based on love is possible.

As previous ages recapitulated earlier ones, so is this the precursor of the future war in heaven depicted in terms of Michael and the dragon (Rev. 12: 7). The battle has begun, and we are all the battleground, whether we wish it or not.

The Being of Christ

It will become increasingly evident from what follows that individual progress, and indeed the whole future of the earth, depends upon mankind's union with the being of Christ. Why is this so important? The name means Messiah, Redeemer; but what is encompassed by it? It is not sufficient, though a starting-point, to recognize—as do all the Churches—that someone named Jesus Christ once lived in Palestine as an outstanding example to humanity (of which there are others).

Christ is in the first place the divine Logos or Cosmic Word, as described by John: 'In the beginning was the Word. And the Word was with God, and the Word was God ... All things became through him, and without him not one thing became which has become.' As a human word consists of consonants and vowels, so the Cosmic Word is expressed through the beings and forces of the fixed stars and the planetary movements. He was moreover the Pleroma or Fullness of the seven Elohim,[8] who said: 'Let us make man in our image, after our likeness' (Gen. 1: 26). We are thus concerned with a fount of creative forces within the world of reality, in the centre of which arises mankind in all its complexity. These forces still manifest in the infant as the distinctively human capacities of walking, speaking and thinking, and then withdraw behind the hereditary (animal) qualities in the blood, where they ameliorate our ill health and can be found again in freedom.

The great religions of the past worshipped Christ—under various names such as Ahura Mazdao, Osiris or Krishna among others—as the great Sun Being, Lord of the solar system. This was a significant stage on his descent to earth. In nature we recognize the sun forces as warmth, light, chemical/sound ether and life. The latter are the Tree of Life, withheld from mankind at the Fall. Inwardly we experience the sun forces as inner light, love and life.

Then the event recorded as the Baptism in Jordan marked the incorporation of this Being, the creative Logos, into a very specially prepared human body, that of Jesus of

Nazareth, for the period of three years described in the Gospels.[9] He thus became visible for once even to the physical senses of mankind. The most important aspect of his incarnation is neither his teaching nor the example he set — vitally significant though both these are — but that he gave his body to the earth. For this body was unique, both in what was brought by Jesus to the Baptism, and especially through the indwelling of Christ, the divine Logos, during the three years.

So far as the living organism of the earth itself is concerned, it thereby became his body — Corpus Christi — and he remains with it to become the Spirit of the Earth.[10] 'I am with you always unto the end of the age' (Matt. 28: 20). The earth thus contains within it both the sun forces through which it will in due course become able to reunite with the sun, and also the impulse for the next planetary evolution.

About the time of Golgotha a crucial change occurred in humanity, expressed in the fact that the dull feeling of self indicated by conjugation of the verb was separated out as a personal pronoun — in Greek, 'ego'. For it was Christ who brought to mankind full self-consciousness, which is indeed universal, beyond the spirit of any one people. As he said: 'Before Abraham was, I am' (John 8: 58). But few have yet understood this. To offset the inherent dangers of egoism he also brought in himself the great gift of that love which extends beyond family and race to all humanity and all things, and will gradually transform the earth itself into a planet of love; but each individual must find this impulse within himself.

Moreover, 'Out of his fullness we all received, and grace upon grace' (John 1: 16). Grace at that time meant the soul's capacity for doing right out of oneself, namely, the capacity of freedom. But the fullness was sevenfold, and thus we have the seven great 'I am' statements of John's Gospel.

In Christ we have the cosmic (heavenly), which descended because spiritual worlds were to be closed to human vision. Thinking deals only with what is past; in nature and culture we find only what leads to death. In a human body alone exists that which bears the future, the eternal spirit. Therefore Christ had to dwell in Jesus of Nazareth and become Christ Jesus.[11] In the seven stages of John's Gospel, it was not Christ who had to develop, but the body of Jesus, pure and noble though it already was. To understand this double being of Christ Jesus is a great task.

Thus there arose for mankind through the forces of the Resurrection a renewed physical form-shape, totally transparent, containing as a kind of germ the creative forces needed for the future, referred to by Paul as 'the incorruptible body' (1 Cor. 15: 42).[12] When multiplied, as if from a single cell, this can now be received by everyone who makes the necessary inner connection with Christ.[13]

The mystery of Christ will only gradually be revealed.

2
The Future of the Fifth Age

The End of Michael's Rulership

By the start of the twenty-third century, when Michael's Sun-rulership as Time Archangel ends (though he continues as Spirit of the Age for more than a millennium) great changes will obviously have taken place.

Firstly, human etheric bodies gradually loosen from the physical, and souls begin to extricate themselves, so that a new experience, that of the Double, is bound to become widespread. The Double consists of everything that is clustered round the ego itself, hitherto invisible to us because we are one with it—our views and opinions, our inclinations and passions, our likes and dislikes, and all our karmic obligations. The 'I' must become able to look on all this as outside itself. Aspects of it, taken hold of by Lucifer and Ahriman and distorted by unschooled astral vision, form the first supersensible experiences, and they can be frightening. Most people cannot understand or cope with them, and descend into the abyss of doubt, anxiety and mental illness. For science, this is 'just another natural development'.

But those who have worked with the impulse of Michael can recognize these experiences. They understand that we become what we are through parents, teachers, friends and, especially perhaps, our apparent enemies; and that our stature depends on the effects we have on others and on the world—not on what we like to think we 'are'. They recognize that their real self lives neither in their own body nor in their thinking, feeling and willing, but in those around them (see p. 45). From this vantage point they are able to go out of themselves and look back from outside saying 'that is not I, but you'. Then they can confront the Double and transform it into the Guardian of the Threshold to the spiritual world. Here the true impulse of Pisces — to give up the everyday ego and receive the 'I' that lives in the periphery — finds expression. The corollary is of course that one becomes conscious of carrying aspects of the being of others within one's own soul.

Realization of this in practice, not only in theory, changes the nature of the community concerned, for then its members can but live one within the other. The visible person is seen as no more than a picture of the spiritual being, with whom one is interwoven through connections formed before birth, and with whom one prepares future lives; and this knowledge lays the foundation of a new morality. Communities of this kind form 'islands of culture' in a hostile world. They are healthy when the whole community is reflected in each single soul, and in the community the strength of each single soul is living.

The actual incarnation of Ahriman, the prince of lies, will by now have taken place, unless Michael, contrary to his usual practice, has himself intervened to defer it. For Michael still fights the Spirits of Darkness until AD 2300. If Ahriman has succeeded in his aims, he will have established an occult school in which pupils are made clairvoyant without the intense effort properly necessary for self-development; but in that case they must each see something different, because they cannot then prevent it from being distorted (without their knowledge) by their unredeemed Double. This must inevitably result in confusion and strife, through which all culture is overthrown.[1] What matters is to confront this situation from the right point of view. More and more people have by now learnt from Michael to intensify their capacity of reasoning and aesthetic judgement (developing the two-petal lotus flower in the brow) until their thoughts become as inwardly alive as the phenomena of nature, which Ahriman, who promulgates dead intellectual thinking, abhors. By 2200/2300 scientific thoughts will no longer have any significance for them.

Moreover those who feel accountable to Christ for everything they do may now acquire new forces through an important experience which has occurred to a very few people since 1933, but will gradually become more widespread. This is the appearing (*epiphaneia*) of Christ himself as an etheric figure in the astral (elemental) world ('dwelling in unapproachable light' – 1 Tim. 6: 14), just as he was once visible to a limited number of people in the physical world. 'Blessed are the pure in heart, for they shall see God' (Matt. 5: 8). Those who take into themselves the growth forces of the plant kingdom, and come to behold the etheric earth, are released from the forces that today hinder such an experience. This is just a first step towards the 'second coming' (p. 61). 'There are a few in Sardis* who have not defiled their sheaths, and they shall walk with me in white, for they are worthy' (Rev. 3: 4).

Also, after death, when the etheric body separates before the soul enters kamaloca, Christ will increasingly be met as karmic judge, as Lord of Karma. One has to gaze on what one has done, and there arises something like a dream-picture of the compensation which must be carried out that best fits with the concerns of the world. And even during life those who feel accountable to Christ will feel a sudden urge to stop what they are doing because of a remarkable vision, a transformation of conscience, which magically forewarns of the compensation it incurs. This form of karma-perception is such that the figure of the etheric Christ, the actual Christ as he lives in the astral world,

---

*Sardis, seat of rich Croesus, twice captured due to careless watch, typifies our fifth age.

becomes directly visible as counsellor and protector of those who need advice, help or solace in the loneliness of their lives. And those who learn through spiritual science the language of Christ can receive from him not only consolation and strength, but in a crisis also illumination and instruction as to what is to be done for the best.[2] Thereby the words 'I am the light of the world' (John 8: 12) become inner experience. For Christ is our brother, who wants to be consulted on all the details of our life. He stands beside us, taking over from us the effects in the cosmos of our misdeeds, leaving us only to compensate for the harm we have done to ourselves.

This will come! But whilst eastern brotherhoods simply wish to prevent it from being noticed, western brotherhoods want also to take over Christ's influence for themselves. Both therefore oppose these developments, and their endeavours must be overcome. Conflict and suffering are therefore inevitable. The Antichrist will even be called 'Christ' by his followers. But all true Christians, knowing that Christ does not incarnate again in physical form but only in the etheric, will oppose him with all the strength at their command, a strength that will be enhanced by practice. This is a very real battle to replace Christ by Ahriman for the remaining 6000 years of the Post-Atlantean epoch.[3]

Oriphiel's Rulership

From the early twenty-third to the late twenty-sixth century the ruling Archangel is Oriphiel, the Archangel of the Saturn sphere. His last rulership from the second century BC to the second century AD was characterized by the decline of Greek culture and the rise of the Roman Empire, which was committed to the elimination of mystery wisdom. Into this came the descent of Christ. And since the ninth century

Oriphiel has led the other Archangels who have sought, since the fall of the cosmic intelligence from Michael, to emancipate themselves from his predominance.

Saturn is not only the preserver of cosmic memory but also the source of human memory. This has steadily deteriorated since ancient times, now to a critical degree. Among those who undertake self-development, however, a new form of memory has been emerging that is more like a looking back on the tableau of past events than the present recall of a single incident, such that past events appear to be separated spatially. And now a delicate organ for remembrance of the previous life is brought generally to completion. From waking to falling asleep the emerging etheric body has dreamy visions of its karma from the past life (which has shaped the personal brain), and during sleep of karma in the making. The retrospect is less concerned with actions and experiences in space, less like a realistic picture, but more like looking back into the life of the soul. Those who today study spiritual science and understand the true nature of the soul crystallize their ego, carry it through death and will be able to recognize it; those who clearly inscribe esoteric thoughts into the Akashic* can use the organ rightly.[4] But those who today do not trouble to comprehend the nature of the individual soul will only be able to recall the group-ego in which they remain. They feel born and educated for a certain way of thinking and visualizing, which however does not fit properly into the world around them, for it comes from the previous life. This discrepancy will give rise in a future life to specific nervous illnesses that will be far worse than any known today.

Ordinary intelligence too becomes something quite different in the future from what it is today, for it is actually the gift of Lucifer, and contains the impulse to become animal.

---

*Objective memory substance of the cosmic ether.

Hence more and more it thinks out only what is evil, wrong and illusory, and brings error into knowledge and evil into moral life. Since thought is exactly the same as electricity, viewed in the one case from within and in the other from without, and since the physical atom is condensed, frozen electricity, people learn to build with atoms through the power of thinking—but also to destroy. Electricity drives out of the nerves everything that tends towards spirit; consequently what is received by radiation (electronically) can no longer be understood.

Man has within him a fiery centre of destruction, of dissolution of matter. The ego is brought into existence by plunging into this chaos of destruction; it must be tempered and hardened there. But if one is not made aware of this centre by spiritual science, it breaks out and permeates the instincts, as seen today.

Many discoveries are made the better to carry on war, and an endless amount of intelligence is used to satisfy the lower impulses. The materialistic outlook continues to advance until AD 2300/2400. The outer world becomes increasingly hostile to human nature, especially what is merely 'useful'. Giant machines, for example, create demons that come alive and rage against the individual. Even machines ought to be created out of joy and beauty.

The forces in flowing water and sunshine are now put to egoistic use. By technical working with the duality of magnetism (the forces of Gemini) human vibrations can bring the cosmos itself into corresponding movement. Through ever-increasing intellectualistic thoughts the warmth-atmosphere of the earth, already under threat, can be ruined. Fiery volcanic (Saturn) outbursts are put to use. And it even becomes possible to turn the axis of the earth.

Dissolute sensuous passions in the great cities today are moreover warning signs of the lurid, hellish glare of yet other adversary beings called Asuras who prompt the ego and consciousness soul to unite wholly with earthly matter. The Spirits of Darkness, who incorporate themselves in bacteria and bacilli, give rise to fear. But through freeing oneself from anxiety, positive forces are developed that are required for Jupiter evolution.

All that takes place in the human organism is however an effect of the great universe—the sun must be in a certain position and so on—and we have only to work our way up to imaginative consciousness. When people become master craftsmen of what is living, machines can be driven by spiritual forces according to spiritual morality. Hence it is the task of the good, healing impulse of this age to find the cosmic forces of Pisces and Virgo, which can now be placed in the service of mankind. One must allow what one does in the morning to be further influenced in the evening, whilst cosmic influences are excluded in between, and again held back until morning, so that a rhythm is created. Such forces engender remarkable machines which bear in themselves a certain force of intelligence.[5] Whereas a good individual can start such machines through sympathetic vibrations produced when he waves his hand this way, that way, another way, evil-minded people produce different vibrations to which the machines do not respond. Thus an entire factory may operate in a completely individual way in keeping with the one who directs it. This develops in a large way among English-speaking peoples.

Saturn forces lie at the foundation of the senses, and it is through them that Oriphiel works to strengthen the lower ego and make the person earthbound. Michael, however, sought during his rulership to form mental images of the spirit, and to establish the relationship of human beings to the cosmos. When therefore his forces of spirit encounter the sense-bound forces of Oriphiel about AD 2300 they are bound to conflict. We are called upon to fight, and mighty conflicts rage, which people have to learn to withstand. A tiny handful of people are being prepared today to keep the torch of spiritual knowledge alight.

If the Mystery of Golgotha were to be rejected, if individuals do not apply to it their own inner forces, souls would have to withdraw from their bodies after the 33rd year. But the soulless bodies with an automatic intellect would live on as a welcome prize for demonic beings. Only the discovery within us of the spark of Christ — the Cosmic Word — and sincere admission of Paul's words 'Not I, but Christ in me' (Gal. 2: 20) can rescue human reasoning.[6] If at least a small number of people cannot now bring the necessary earnestness to this situation, further human evolution would not be possible. This is a very serious matter.[7]

These terrible times are far worse than today. They produce no seed and no harvest, but may be regarded as a premature expression of divine wrath. Saturn forces tend to form boundaries, and we see here a clear boundary between those who work with progressive forces and those who do not.

Anael's Rulership

Those alive today can expect their next incarnation after 700/800 years (though there are wide exceptions; those with lower instincts or making a sacrifice come sooner). The ruling Archangel is then Anael, the Venus Archangel, whose last rulership from the mid-second to the fifth century was characterized by countless deeds of love, such as those of the Irish monks, and by vast migrations from east to west. Experiencing their gods within, it was as if they were driven by an inner urge for outer discovery. This now turns to inner discovery, for the Venus mood is mysticism, quietly seeking for divine light. Venus fills the soul with ideals and religious impulses, and gives rise to great deeds of self-sacrificial love, a foretaste of the future Venus evolution. It is also the realm of Active Soul Force, the source of powerful artistic impulses which create things of beauty and lift the beholder to the spirit. This is therefore a much better time, which sees a renewal of cosmic life on earth and inspires inner spiritual strength.

From this time on, intellectuality becomes increasingly paralysed by immorality; so that a person without morals has no intellectual powers, for these come to depend entirely on moral actions.[8] The gap between ordinary abstract thinking and the reasoning capacity of the consciousness soul which lives in imaginative pictures grows wider.

Everyone in the civilized world has an instinctive feeling for socialism until the fourth millennium, not as a party-political matter but because the feeling for it is latent not in the soul but in the temperament, the subconscious. But antisocial forces also continue to increase until the thirtieth century, the end of Anael's rule — they are necessary for the assertion of self, which is the task of the fifth Post-Atlantean age. Only when a person's labour is no longer sold — actually an insult to the individual akin to slavery — but simply directed where it is needed can antisocial feelings be mitigated.

If in 2800 or 3000 we look back on today, we should thoroughly despise ourselves if we had confused moral strength and a resolute will for freedom — inner freedom in the first place, then outer freedom soon follows — with our love of ease and comfort, and the indulgence of benevolent gods. Materialists, for example, today regarded as authorities, will now find their brains too soft to serve for thinking.

Zachariel's Rulership

Zachariel, the Archangel of the Jupiter sphere, is due to hold the rulership from the early thirtieth to the late thirty-third century. His last rule, from the sixth to the mid-ninth century, was not so fully developed as some, but saw the rise of personal intelligence, especially in the form of Arabism, which was spiritually dead, in place of the earlier thinking inspired by Angelic beings. Jupiter, which delimits the Oceanic region of Spiritland where the germs of the etheric arise, now brings forces of wisdom, and with the mood of Logicism a new unity and harmony of thought, a foretaste of the future Jupiter evolution (p. 114). But first at the end of the third millennium Ahriman and Lucifer again hold sway.

With the steady emergence of the etheric body, one feels oneself growing into and receiving impressions from an entirely different world from that of the senses, and by now an entirely new spirituality must have been established. More and more people develop naturally the clairvoyant power to see the etheric body, the etheric aura and rays (at least as a shadowy image), and to perceive the relationship in the etheric world between all profounder events, or to see pictures or premonitions of events that will occur in a few days' time. This does not reach completion before AD 4500, but through esoteric training it can be acquired earlier and in far better form, and to let it pass would be a misfortune.[9] This is the real 'healing of the man born blind' by him who said 'I am the light of the world' (John 8:12).

What we see as a person is now recognized as mere picture (p. 27). We come nearer to the reality in the feelings of warmth or cold they evoke. Waking consciousness itself is experienced as an intimate fire process that consumes us. This is a product of the twelve-petal lotus flower in the heart.

The other side of this ongoing process involves forming a new relationship to the forces of death. Already today, modern thinking, especially in its demand for experimental proof, can only comprehend the corpse of reality, the death element. In constructing our machines, in submitting people to the discipline of machines, we introduce the forces of death into social life. Already people go about with death at their side, and now they see how death works on them all the time. By 3500 everyone must and can completely unite their own being with its forces, the real function of which is to endow one with the capacity to develop the consciousness soul — death itself is only a kind of side-effect.[10] For those who have awoken the eternal forces of the soul, death is indeed a friend — as the Manichaeans knew — for it frees us from the physical world.

For an actual realization of the Christ experience one must have a sure conviction of the life of the soul after death, and of the fact that one then works down spiritually onto the physical world — the very facts of life compel people to take account of such things. Therefore it is now important to know also that when we work with others we do so together with the dead. Those who have died know better than the living what must happen socially, and the living have to become instruments to put their knowledge into practice. *No well-being can come in certain spheres unless the dead are consulted,* and this fact must now be grasped not only in thought but in feeling and will, and applied in life.

Thus the whole way of beholding changes. The activity of the cosmos on the earth is recognized — the working of the stars within the plant kingdom, the working of the sun through the whole Platonic year in the colours of the minerals. People in 2900 no longer think about the solar system as they do today! This is all part of a progressive change, without which the next step in evolution is not possible. The consciousness soul can only unfold because the forces that will later be fully developed on Jupiter already throw their shadow ahead.

If instead the forces of the West were to spread over the whole earth, the urge would arise to extinguish what has been won in freedom, and to revert to primitive conditions and primitive clairvoyance.[11] Most people would have little interest in worldly affairs compared to enobling their own souls to see into the spiritual world. A small group, however, would seize power over large masses of people, and suppress by inoculations in childhood those qualified to prepare for the sixth epoch.[12] Information relating to human propagation, illness and death may be used for either good or evil, making possible a far-reaching influence on human affairs.

If however Central Europe were to dominate the whole earth, people would be yoked to the course of the year, to all that lives in wind and weather, and terrible egoism would result. And if the forces rightly in the East were to spread over the whole, everything connected with the atmosphere and the stars would be eliminated from civilization. The planetary system would be compelled to vibrate along with the clatter and rattle of the earth. And the East itself would remain in childhood, leaving the physical body unused.

Raphael's Rulership

The end of our fifth Post-Atlantean age ruled by Michael is reached in 3573, towards the end of Raphael's rulership. He last predominated from the mid-ninth to the twelfth century, when humanity was already sick in soul through materialism. But Raphael, the Mercury Archangel, is the great cosmic physician, and through his impulse of Christendom and the development of personal feelings, moral qualities were greatly healed.

By the end of this age, every individual must in some measure have passed the Guardian of the Threshold. Those who take serious pains to learn about the spiritual world pass consciously. But those who are still afraid of the spiritual life, because the animal in them is afraid, meet the Guardian in the subconscious and their fear increases. The latter confront Ahriman's cold intellectual thoughts in their nerves and head, and to balance this they have to take Lucifer into themselves in order to press down everything that the over-strong ego has accumulated there into the rest of the organism. In doing so they experience inner tragedies such as those of Faust, and can only break free by striving to expand their consciousness into the spiritual world and deepening their knowledge of spiritual events. For the real concept of the human being lies inherently beyond the Threshold; and the ego must grasp that it is a citizen of the spiritual world, not just of the body.[13]

Among the forces of the six Elohim brought to earth by Christ (Jehovah having a separate task on the moon) it is just those of healing which are his special gift to our fifth age[14] — were it not so, our bodies today would already be much more decayed than they are. Immersion in any sense-free ideas — whether mathematics, religion or spiritual science — facilitates the healing of this inner sickness. But this healing cannot be fully grasped until it is realized that nature itself is a process of creative art, which can only be understood by artistic feeling. And it is Raphael who works here with the healing forces of Mercury, especially in the processes of breathing and circulation. Understanding the source of pathological symptoms then depends on looking outwards towards the cosmic rhythms. Mercury, messenger of the gods, represents the whole second part of Earth evolution, for he leads people out of the sense world to the spiritual beings revealed in the stars. This will culminate in the union of science, art and religion in a single whole, preferably in a work of art whose elements are a sequence of sounds. A symbolic indication of such a sequence exists in Wagner's *Parsifal*.

Love based on physical relationships, the basis of tribalism and racialism, now comes to an end, and present differences between civilized and primitive people also cease. But love for an individual outside the family, first possible in the fourth age, now becomes *love for a whole group of people*. 'He who loves father or mother … son or daughter more than me is not worthy of me' (Matt. 10: 37). That is why no happiness is possible for anyone alone without that of everyone in the group.

People will live in groups which they create for themselves by allowing their feelings to stream together with those of similar ideas, while retaining their complete freedom and individuality – the anthroposophical society is intended to be a first example, and there will be many more based on intellectual-ethical-moral aspects. And the more such groups come together freely, the more can lofty beings descend into them as a new kind of voluntary group soul, and the more rapidly can the earth be spiritualized. For 'supermen' of Vulcan, Venus, Mercury and the sun are even today descending from the sphere between the moon and Mercury, intending to unite with such groups. If they are opposed, catastrophes must ensue and the earth pass into chaos – an automatic intellect could develop even amid conditions of barbarism.[15]

Meanwhile more and more people experience the phenomena surrounding the appearance of Christ in the etheric world, which do not reach their culmination until the end of the fifth millennium. And nations of the northern part of the East are preparing something like a mighty marriage of spiritual thinking with the intellectuality of the West; but this can only be of value if the German Folk Spirit can find souls able to graft the Christ impulse into their astral bodies quite consciously, and this must be visualized as taking to AD 3500. It would be the greatest misfortune if Germany were to injure that power which it ought to cultivate with devotion and friendship.[16]

*   *   *

This whole age, when the Threshold is crossed, may be compared to the event of death in the individual, and also to the advent of cosmic life. It is the metamorphosis of intellectual thinking to living, imaginative thinking that is of prime importance.

What results must be the seed, not only for the sixth age, but also for the subsequent sixth epoch, because the sixth and seventh ages belong to a descent. This seed is recruited from all races of the world; it must experience enmity and persecution, but everywhere some people work to bind humanity together. Through those who dedicate themselves to this great brotherhood a remedy is provided for the others who live thoughtlessly and turn a deaf ear to spiritual science. The transformation even to the sixth age, when Michael is no longer Spirit of the Age, can only occur through great tumultuous catastrophes, great physical upheavals, for that must already be something radically different.

We must never forget that we must be fighters for the spirit. Our forces grow slack unless kept constantly in training for conquest of the spirit. We now depend on freedom, and must experience it fully. If our energies turn slack, everything might turn to evil.[17] 'He who overcomes shall be clothed in white (the soul image of the spirit) and by no means shall I blot out his name from the book of life, but will acknowledge it before my father and his angels' (Rev. 3: 5).

3
The Sixth Age

The New Conditions

The sixth Post-Atlantean cultural age, the so-called Russian age, extends from 3573 to 5733. It is also known as the Aquarian age, because it is prepared and guided by forces from the Waterman, where the vernal point stands from 2375 to 4535. These are etheric forces of rejuvenation, resurrection and rebirth, but if not turned to the spirit they can lead to dissolution. This age is represented in the Apocalypse as Philadelphia (Rev. 3: 7–13). As the etheric body continues to withdraw from the physical and expand into the cosmos, vision of the etheric world increases, and the whole experience of the environment changes. Material culture has now to be united with life in the spiritual world. A kind of break with the past, a new spiral of existence is to be brought about, though the new impulses are at first germinal, awkward, unskilful compared with the old, which is clear-cut but destructive.

First, the Double (pp. 26–27) must be fully recognized and overcome. This age is centred in Russia because Russian soil reflects back special forces in the cosmic light which awaken the capacity to do this (there is no leading race as such). The Slavonic Folk Spirit works in this vibrating light to affect the way in which ideas are formed in the head, and in which heart and lung work upwards to meet them. Since the ninth century Russians have been specially prepared through Arius and the Goths as a 'People of Christ' for whom Christ is spirit. Then through Russian Orthodoxy their temperament was fed by the classical Greek Spirit of the Age. But a continuation from this is no longer possible — a leap must be made. The Russian lays more importance on direct connection with an individual person than on what is written, and his greatest gift lies in absorbing things, especially from Central Europe. The role of the Russian soul thus depends on whether or not the essential reality of the Grail, the linking of the inmost awakening of the individual's spiritual soul with the spiritual world, becomes a cultural ferment for the whole world.

The natural growth and development of the human being, which today continues to age 27, stops at 21 at the start of this age, and does not reach beyond 14 by its end. The body, including to a diminishing extent the sentient body, therefore still develops naturally, but not the soul, unless the individual develops it for himself from within through the ego. Outer education never achieves more than the body, so juvenile schizophrenia is epidemic. And one cannot make good, even after death, what is let slip, unless one receives spiritual stimulus.[1] Furthermore, reproduction in its present form, depending as it does upon puberty, ceases to occur naturally at the end of this age.

The intellect, increasingly used for bodily or warlike needs, is now experienced as an entity spread outside the soul (a world-wide web), much more objectively powerful than it is today. So one has to submit to it, and Ahriman constantly seeks to take possession of it. At first, material scientists consider those who strive for truth through spiritual science to be ill, and administer medicines compulsorily to anyone who holds that there is an objective standard of good and evil, that these are anything more than man-made categories to be varied at will. Materialists find their exclusive pleasure in living on what is brought about by bacilli, tuberculi etc. that corrode the corpse of the earth. Thoughts that remain purely intellectualistic instead of being transformed to Imagination poison not only the warmth but the air, *ruining all vegetation*; even bread and wine — the symbol of the fourth age — have to be given up. Those animals which supply our food, whose forms are the most rigid (but not all animals) also die out. Before then, however, purely mineral nourishment can be produced in the laboratory, which in turn lays the foundation for the future capacity for self-reproduction (p. 55).

But materialistic science and belief come to be regarded as an antiquated superstition, and only knowledge based on the spirit is accepted. Physical configurations of sun and stars lose significance when the powerful ruling and interweaving of the spirits expressed in them become visible. And collective beliefs such as those of religion no longer influence civilized humanity — everyone feels that complete freedom of thought in this field is a fundamental right of each individual. Anyone who still believes that the physical world is the only reality, having lost all relationship to the loosening etheric body and lost his bearings in the spiritual world, and having no ground under his feet but fantasy, illusion and a world in whose true reality he does not believe, then finds himself for all time dangling in mid-air, threatened with what is known as 'spiritual death'.[2] The struggle will be bitter before the Christ impulse can be brought through.

The body is then understood as a spiritual being of divine origin, whose muscles, for example, are moved directly by the cosmic harmony resounding in the astral body.* Christianity makes the body softer and more malleable, so that as thoughts grow stronger they mould the heart into an organ through which one can voluntarily control the whole body, carrying soul impulses out into the world or withdrawing them. Its fibres are already striated for this purpose. When the wisdom that has been prepared through Saturn, Sun and Moon lives in such a body and is resurrected in the inner life, it grows into the seed of love.

---

* How else a piano recital? (RGS)

The forces of form that originate in selfless thoughts and feelings, especially those deriving from real wisdom, assume ever greater importance for the outward appearance of individuals all over the earth. Physical bodies copy the etheric more closely than before, so that they express directly the inner moral qualities, and heredity becomes irrelevant. From strongly marked features, which neither religion nor education can alter, others can perceive one's moral constitution; and this may constitute an almost fatal destiny. Only through treating the etheric world as very real and earnest, and taking up through spiritual science the etheric shape of Christ, can corrections be made.[3] Nevertheless, one cannot always judge an individual in this way; for a person who is thoroughly good may take over and incarnate in a body destined for evil prepared by someone they have perhaps injured, and enable them to enter that which they had prepared for themselves. Such people consider what is best for humanity—that is 'white magic'.[4]

The Awakening of the 'I'

The spiritual outlook of Aquarius is Pneumatism, which means that the spirit is active as thinker. Living thinking becomes a real force, and great masses of people are deeply moved and seized by truths which are today revealed only to a few. The truths of anthroposophy will of course, after 2500–3000 years, be experienced and expressed in completely different forms, namely, as Imaginations.*

The impulse of Christ now works through the Eloha of Seership, which is needed for life within the Spirit Self. This

---

*Everything is created out of astral images. When mental images are filled with life from the side of the spirit, they become Imaginations. This is not perfected until Jupiter. See further *An Outline of Occult Science*, V.

age is related to ours as is a spiritually minded soul to one intellectually inclined, so that genuine Christianity recognizes the external world as condensed spirit. It brings genius, clairvoyance and the creative spirit to development; and people notice the etheric tension where a genius lives. The task is first to have the spiritual world continually in view, and to live in accordance with it; and then to popularize esoteric truth in the widest circles, to carry it right into life and put it into practice everywhere. There is in fact no other way of bringing about universal human brotherhood — talking (preaching) about love is clearly insufficient, and now leads only to egoism.[5] The ideal of this age is thus practical wisdom, which Plato called 'justice', meaning the harmonious accord of truth, love and moderation. Understanding of the highest principles can come much later. The picture in Luke's Gospel of the development of Jesus of Nazareth will be a special help.

Today the ego is ordinarily experienced in the intellectual soul as mere reflection within the body — few perceive its reality. But now it is normally experienced outside the body through the spiritual soul (p. 26). Those who form the kernel of the age all over the earth have been well prepared by anthroposophy to remember their individual 'I', which enables them in freedom to show love to all other beings.

As the result of this awakening 'at' the others (not merely 'to' them) we feel their suffering or need, their poverty, as our own, right down to the physical body, so that it is unendurable. Every person we meet then has more to do with our 'I' than anything within our own skin. Then the well-being of the individual really does depend on that of the whole community; a common consciousness lays hold. Through altruistic thinking, spiritual relationships replace blood relationships. Knowledge becomes a social force, and for the first time Christianity becomes the shaper of a new social order.

Once sufficient people experience themselves as citizens of the cosmos, social life is transformed. All that people do becomes an offering to the community, remuneration is separated from work, and everything is held as common property instead of in private ownership. All that Rudolf Steiner has said about the threefolding of the social order can now be realized. This is a preparation for the sixth epoch. A community where higher things have become second nature, where souls are fully permeated with enthusiasm for the true and beautiful, where it is realized that justice should prevail, and where enthusiasm for good is reality, manifests the Christian ideal of brotherhood which is on the path towards Life Spirit. The sixth letter of the Apocalypse (Rev. 3: 7–13) is addressed to such a community.

Characteristic of this time are very definite feelings of morality and immorality drawn from Lower Spiritland, of whose intensity we cannot today have the faintest conception. Delicate feelings of sympathy are aroused by compassionate, kindly deeds, and of antipathy by malicious actions. One takes pleasure in good and noble deeds, displeasure in evil. The virtue of Aquarius is discretion, which is enhanced to meditative force (otherwise it degenerates into lewdness, which makes moral progress impossible). Our age which demands rights is thus succeeded by one which asks after tasks.

Nevertheless when a person does wrong, not only is it written into their own karma, but another person or group can help them, conscientiously accepting their destiny and seeking to improve it. Thus with every 'forgiveness of sins' the community recognizes its responsibility, and individual karma is interwoven with community karma according to the pattern of the heavenly order.[6] Knowledge of karma then becomes actual reality, selfhood and selflessness are held in balance, and one neither loses oneself in the world nor encloses oneself in egoism.

The Reception of Spirit Self

It is the task of this age to receive the Spirit Self, not into the entire astral body, which is not possible on earth, but into the spiritual soul. It can however descend only in a community of the kind described, where brotherhood, freedom of thought and spiritual science prevail, and wine is not taken. Here the Russian capacity for receptivity comes into play. In past ages Spirit Self was directly perceived like a star soaring above a person's head, and was called the guiding genius or 'daimon'. Today it is enclosed in the bosom of our angel, who is of like nature to it. But during every long sleep we already encounter it unconsciously in the astral aura, rayed down from him as our eternal being, which slowly changes us and, as we refine our spiritual life, we may sense this in feelings which gladden our soul on waking.

Spirit Self is on the one hand the astral body transformed by the ego so that there are no more unguarded impulses, instincts or passions. On the other hand it is only a different expression for what Steiner calls in his philosophy 'pure thinking' or higher thinking,[7] with which comes immersion in a common wisdom. It is a condensation of what is today esoteric knowledge into a 'cognition body'. Cosmically the Spirit Selfhood lies behind the stars as the whole world of the Hierarchies. When there is agreement about higher reality as there is today about mathematics, then in the strengthened individuality the inmost kernel is felt as the most universal. This union of 'I' and Spirit Self was called in esoteric Christianity a spiritual marriage: 'On the third day (4–5–6th age) there was a marriage in Cana'; but at that time 'My time is not yet come' (John 2: 1).

Christ however also taught his intimate disciples that the temple of the 'I' in its present form must be killed, and after a rhythm of three days (determined by cosmic laws) must rise again (John 2: 19).[8] This was the Mystery experience of 'dying and becoming'. First the astral body has to be cleansed, purified, ennobled and subjected to catharsis, and thus transformed to what is called in esoteric Christianity the Virgin Sophia. This then is illumined from above — overshadowed — by the Cosmic Ego, called the Holy Spirit.[9]

Spirit Self thus does not enter without deep inner tragedy, suffering and soul drama. Having been taught in childhood to feel something entering that has gone through death and come again, the spiritual soul feels the intellectual soul as the direct killer of its thoughts, the inner thought-murderer. A certain tiredness, dullness first comes over one, one becomes empty. Then divine thoughts stream in and spread over the grave: Spirit Self comes.[10] The mood must therefore be 'Thy Kingdom Come' — a kingdom not of this world but of the spiritual world.

When Spirit Self draws into human beings, they thus become immersed in a common wisdom. They begin to feel that their inmost kernel coincides exactly with that in another, their real being interpenetrates. There is but one reality. A spiritual sun is actually present towards which all men incline, and in which they become harmonized. This union is thus the guarantee for true peace and brotherhood — there is then no more strife. Hence 'Blessed are the peacemakers (those who draw down Spirit Self): they shall be called the children of God' (Matt. 5: 9). Moreover the gradual replacement of intellectual thoughts by such universal thoughts of the Spirit Self represents also the gradual redemption of Lucifer (p. 96).

Already today the higher self lives around us, not within us, and can be developed by immersing oneself in inspired writings. In a few thousand years the self becomes what is now the higher self.[11] Every progressive soul comes to be spread out over the movements of the macrocosm, creates itself from the wisdom of the great universe, and looks from there upon the body towards which it is focused. It is essential to know that twelve different aspects can be seen of every single 'I'; only then have we a complete picture of it. An individual who develops his 'I' in the spiritual soul in such a way actually forms a cavity in his soul; through the qualities with which it then endows heart and blood he experiences for the first time its purity as a receptacle; and into this receptacle Christ can enter. But it is essential that the integration of thinking, feeling and willing be now under the full control of the 'I'.

Already before 4000 AD people in whom a large part of the so-called forces of evil have been transformed begin to hear the soul of the other through their words. This brings a different configuration of feeling, a different form of living together. In listening not to the content but to the gesture of the other's language, which discloses their relation to the beings of the Third Hierarchy, a peculiar sensation of colour arises from the sounds.[12] This comes from the development of the ten-petal lotus flower.

Those however who have rejected the Christ impulse, the source of true individuality, necessarily fall back into group souls — people who want to do as 'they' do, want ideas in common with others. These are not the voluntary groupings entered in freedom, but a fearful shackle. To be hemmed in, unable to transcend the group nature, to be directed as to how one should think, feel or act — that is felt as a Fall, as something terrible. Even if these group souls are finer and higher than those of the animals, they are but group souls.[13] This sixth age, the simple '6', can already be fateful to many who persist in materialism; but turning to Christ is still possible.

Christ and the Maitreya

Leading up to the middle of this age, some time about 4300 to 4700, it is the turn of Michael (now an Archon but no longer Spirit of the Age) to act again as the ruling Time Archangel; so a further enhancement of the Christ impulse may then be expected. By now many people have made the eightfold path of Buddha their own in its modern form, which leads through conscious exercises to the unfolding of the 16-petal lotus flower in the larynx. The entire life of feeling is an inward activity of this organ, which outwardly becomes the sense of Inspiration. Whereas knowledge of compassion and love came from Gautama Buddha, the power really to live within it came from Christ, healing through the Word. But when love is united with the power of Buddha and the cosmic mysteries, it becomes something different again. Speech now conveys the aesthetic feelings of the heart from soul to soul.

Feelings then become even a factor in science. If one cannot unfold sufficient feeling or emotion to perceive the world of spirit that brings everything into existence, one fails one's examination. The laboratory bench becomes an altar, and the question is whether feelings comparable to those which the gods experience arise there.[14] Genius, clairvoyance, the creative spirit continue to develop, until mechanical science too is raised to the heights of creative spiritual power. Thus are science and faith reunited.

Most people can now perceive to a greater or lesser extent the etheric Christ as an Angel-like being (p. 28). And as we saw (p. 45), they can say: my self is out there with all those I meet who have anything to do with me; least of all is it within me. In fact we become hollow, and we become Christ-bearers precisely when Christ descends into this hollow space within us.

Once this new 'I' is experienced across the Threshold in reality, no external power can affect us if we do not wish it. It is accordingly known as the Key of David: 'Thus saith ... he that has the Key of David ... Behold I have set before you an open door, and no man can shut it' (Rev. 3: 7). We also have the next great statement of Christ himself: 'I am the door; if anyone enters through me he will be saved' (John 10: 9).

Now occurs the majestic event when Christ is seen to walk the earth, neither in physical nor in etheric form but in an astral body, as pure spiritual form: the Son of Fire and Light of the Earth is revealed in Lower Spiritland.[15]

From his body of light he sends forth into receptive souls as an astral form the Word that was active 'in the Beginning', as described in the opening verses of John's Gospel. Human beings are thus increasingly permeated by the Being of Christ not only as a subject of deep meditation but in all reality. Pure Akashic forms, bathed in fire in the light of the sun, manifest as the retinue of Christ. This whole event is described by Paul in the words: '... the *revelation* (*apokalypsis*) of the Lord Jesus from heaven with his mighty angels in flaming fire' (2 Thess. 1: 7). It is the second step towards the 'second coming'; and John the Baptist will again be a forerunner.

Furthermore, just 5000 years after the elevation of Gautama Buddha, namely, about 4467, the Maitreya Bodhisattva, who comes to earth in every century, will be elevated to Maitreya Buddha ('Buddha of right-mindedness'). He comes now to teach what those wonderful imaginative forms of pure fire and light really are. He speaks in a language for which the physical instrument does not today exist, enabling morality to work magically into hearts and souls directly, like a healing medicine. His utterances are filled in a miraculous way with the power of Christ.[16] In him the power of the Word manifests to an inconceivable degree — the flesh is made Word. Every word is at the same time a moral power. Even his outer life is patterned on that of Christ — he will appear 'between 30 and 33', and will in a certain sense have to imitate what came to pass in the event of Golgotha. Before 30 he is unknown, working through his own power; then he sacrifices his individuality and another individuality dwells in him. Any claim made before that age must be false.

Christ then flows substantially into the air we breathe. Indeed, whether or not Jupiter can follow depends on whether we just release the air again as dead, or whether we unite esoteric knowledge with it and weave the fruits into our own astral body, transforming that further to Spirit Self. A person's moral or immoral nature is actually visible in the etheric-astral content of the out-breath, the forms of which are the first shadowy images of the beings who will reach the human level on Jupiter.

From this time onward people begin to learn to adapt their breathing to one another. They thereby experience the configuration of feeling of the other, and thus know with what kind of person they are dealing. This faculty of Inspiration* already enables people of all nations to come to some understanding of each other.[17] The word must acquire creative force, as it was 'in the beginning'. In the sixth or seventh millennium one's word has as much power on the external world as has the plant seed today. As the physical world loses its importance, people realize that the physical body is merely the grave. The grave is empty, but he who lay within it is risen. For Christ bestows abundant creative power, inspiring and permeating art, and giving strength to discover one's firm centre amongst the gods who are once again beheld.

Many now feel within them the same powerful emotions that Zarathustra evoked when he pointed to Ahura-Mazda,

---

*Inspirations arise within us as tones reflected by our feelings from utterances by beings of the Hierarchies by means of movements in the solar system ('the harmony of the spheres'). It is not perfected until Venus. See further *An Outline of Occult Science*, Chapter V.

and again recognize Christ as the Sun Being, yet now within the soul, and infinitely more sublimely and intimately than before. Indeed this whole age has been guided by those Archangels, already filled by Christ, who guided the ancient Persian culture; and now they show how Christ spiritualizes the whole solar system. When the Magi reappear, community life is again regulated in a way fruitful for karma.

This age in fact recapitulates the Persian (Gemini) age, especially its experience of the polarities between light and dark, good and evil, which is now an actual division between good and evil races. The age is prepared through the sixth sign of Christ, the raising of Lazarus. Those who have not yet taken in Christ, however, are depicted in the parable of the other Lazarus as the rich man who lived in surfeit, but comes to hell (Luke 16: 19). The polarization is not resolved.

The new Christianity of the sixth age has as its symbol the Rose Cross. To the lasting union of calm wisdom with the fire of the astral world (passion and desire) is added the secret of Spirit Self, Life Spirit and Spirit Man with all that it entails, including knowledge of reincarnation and karma. The higher self becomes an open secret, and strife is for the moment resolved.

At the end of this age, the Word — Christ — is present not only in individuals but also in the whole. Single individuals form the letters of the Word. Christ is then in quite another sense the Resurrected One. Those who develop selflessness, awakening in the 'I', are already seeds not just for the seventh age but for the sixth epoch. 'Because you keep my word with fortitude, I will keep you from the hour of trial of those that live on earth ... He that overcomes I will make a pillar in the temple of my God, and he shall by no means be born longer' (Rev. 3: 10).

4
The Seventh Age

A Culture of Will

This age extends from 5733 to about 7900. It is the age of Laodicea: 'I know your deeds, that you are neither cold nor hot. Would that you were!' (Rev. 3: 15). It is not an advance on the sixth age, but rather a regression like an over-ripe fruit, of very little importance in general since it contains no principle of progress. A kind of hypertrophy comes about.

Bodily changes completely alter the human situation. As mentioned on page 42, the age to which natural development extends becomes ever lower. At the start of this age it stops at 14, but by the end it reaches only to seven. Consequently, if evolution were to take its rightful course, women would be barren from the beginning — people would no longer incarnate in bodies derived from physical parents. But due to impulses from America through which the Spirits of Darkness cast down in the 1840s become regents of propagation, this may be deferred to the seventh millennium or a little later. That would however by no means be good for those concerned, because they would become more animal-like.[1] Unless individuals undertake through an inner impulse the development of their own souls, an epidemic of infantilism is inevitable. In contrast, the European East unfolds strong inclinations not to permit sexual propagation to continue, but rather to lead over to an existence more of the nature of soul and spirit.[2] The forces of sex thus released are not just wasted; passions, for example, are transformed to fantasy, and later to Imagination. For the average person today, all this may only be half a dozen incarnations ahead.

Instead, *the larynx becomes the organ for asexual reproduction*, chaste and pure, which turns to the spiritual ray of wisdom for fructification, bringing forth in its own image. Today when we speak, thought is expressed in air vibrations, but what one speaks remains in the Akashic Record, one propagates oneself spiritually. Thought in general expresses itself in forms such as crystals. But one can progress to a living thinking and a living speech that calls forth in what is fluid pictures like living plant forms. It later becomes possible, with the help of the pituitary body (originally the regulator of the moon forces in respiration) to speak forth as radiations ensouled feeling beings in the warmth element—what was said on page 51 of the Maitreya Buddha and the lotus flower in the larynx in connection with the heart refers to this. At the highest stage, by means of the developed pineal gland (originally the organ for fertilization by the sun's warmth), consciously directed willing gives form to the word, externalizing what is willed, continues to live within it, and penetrates the image with the very substance and reality of being.[3] Thus man speaks forth man. As 'in the beginning was the Word, and the Word was a God' (John 1: 1), so now the word is man, and man is a word.

Those who grasp the best possibilities are for a further 2500 years* astir as beings of soul and spirit in the clouds, in rain, in lightning and thunder, in the affairs of the earth; they pulse through the manifestations of nature. 'Except a man be born of water and air (*pneuma*) he cannot enter the kingdom of heaven' (John 3: 5). To achieve this effectively depends on acquiring by about AD 6000 a higher, universal stellar consciousness, a living one's way into the spatial world around one and into one's previous incarnation. This

---

*Perhaps a recording error for 7500 years? (RGS)

is known as Intuition.* And only by becoming conscious today of this process will one now have the power needed. Otherwise, 'because you are lukewarm, I will spew you forth out of my mouth' (Rev. 3: 16).

Progressive souls thus relate to the spiritual world through the will; the moral aspect predominates. When Intuition is now developed it ushers in a Cosmic New Year of 12,000 years in which the forces of Higher Spiritland work in with special strength, bringing not just pleasure in good deeds but firm resolves to *do* what is moral, to follow an active moral life. Moral strength is of a magnitude inconceivable today, and speech is able to transmit moral values from soul to soul. When people develop the power, when their coat is stolen, really to give up their cloak also, there will be no more stealing. Each moral act must become a miracle, not a natural reaction.[4]

Moral and cognitional forces now combine, so that cleverness without morality no longer exists. Intellect alone burns and consumes, enfeebling a person so that he becomes stupid, able to do nothing, and powerless to harm. The secret of secrets is to regard our deeds, not our 'I', as the criterion; the 'I' must remain concealed. Where such a strong morality exists, people group themselves according to their own positive point of view, so that a wonderful harmony arises, based on the division of labour and equality of rights. People know that they must cooperate for the sake of society as a whole, and voluntarily divide according to their morality and intellect. This recalls the castes of the Indian age, but no one is now forced into a caste, and all are equally valued.

---

* Intuition (in a technical sense) is an identifying of the will with individual members of the Hierarchies by means of love. It leads to a cosmic consciousness reaching beyond the solar system. See further *An Outline of Occult Science*, Chapter V.

When one belongs to such a community through one's will, through Intuition, one has to 'digest' the other person, an inner experience comparable to eating (a faculty not fully developed until Vulcan).[5] 'If anyone hears my voice and opens the door, I will come in to him and dine with him, and he with me' (Rev. 3: 20). Meanwhile souls who in the sixth age were carried up into the spiritual world, purified and Christ-ened, walk as it were etherically, no longer touching the earth. Those who did not reach the goal of the sixth age find little opportunity to make up lost ground.

The first Indian age, when the etheric body was to a great extent still outside the physical, is indeed reflected in the seventh, but in only a minority is it Christianized. The Archai (Spirits of Personality) who inspired the Seven Holy Rishis and have since absorbed Christ now lead again. Knowledge leads to perception of the thoughts of the gods whence the world sprang forth, for which the highest feelings of holy awe and reverence are required. The forces for this were given in the raising of Jairus' daughter — despite a great crowd around her, and a flute-player (typically Indian), he goes to her and she is raised by his hand (Matt. 9: 23).[6]

Quite special efforts are again needed to gain a knowledge of nature — colours, for example, are no longer perceived accurately as they are today, and the sense of hearing especially will have practically disappeared. But one who does fully enter the sense world, and who also wrestles with what is revealed in his own soul, again realizes that both lead to a unity ('thou art that'). Everything the Rishis once proclaimed thus comes to pass in great glory and majesty in the most advanced, who are illumined, inflamed, set on fire by the Christ impulse. But now it lives in their souls as their very own, the truth they live by. The Rishis rise again in the splendour of the Christ Sun.

The Ending of Our Epoch

The age as a whole is dominated by Anglo-American culture, led by an abnormal Spirit of Personality who does not work for the progress of evolution. America's endeavour is to mechanize everything, and gradually to extinguish the culture of Europe—this cannot be otherwise, for the magnetic and sub-earthly electric streams of force are specially strong there, and affect the physical organizing forces as forces of decline and death. These work most strongly into the Double, and Europe can only come to a right relationship with America when this is understood.[7]

The true mission of the American people, whilst acquiring world dominion, is to listen to others and learn to interpret the gesture of language, searching for the spiritual being that works directly from etheric body to etheric body. But world egoism also proceeds from the English-American people; through their inventions they cover the earth with a network of egoism fraught with evil. Hence the age has been called a premature birth, one that makes outwardly real too soon and too strongly what should result only later from Spirit Self. As a kind of excess this hardens into egoism, so that this people heads for downfall and rigidification, and within it is the seed of the evil race of the whole next epoch.[8]

This dominating egoism causes the desolation and drying up of regions where it is most pursued, since the withering of souls is connected with paralysis of productive force. There is consequently a revolution of the elements analogous to that which put an end to Atlantis. For where thoughts are not vitalized, giving back to the cosmos what has been received from it, but remain purely intellectual, human exudations pass into the universal fluidity and contaminate the water element; and the mineral loses cohesion—there is every chance of shattering the earth.[9]

Powerful, mighty forces are also discovered that transform the entire earth into a sort of self-functioning electrical apparatus. The earthly has to be left behind, with people directing and controlling it from outside, like an object one need not carry over into cosmic existence. One must so prepare that one need not be involved in what must inevitably develop in this way.

Because by this time sufficient souls have the power to use the moon forces for the benefit of evolution, *the moon again unites with the earth* in the eighth millennium, i.e., towards the end of this age. Naturally this must not be taken as though they would collide.[10] It has already begun to approach the earth, though science must declare reunion to be impossible according to known data; but it cannot envisage the activity of spiritual beings. It was Jehovah who led the moon beings to separate from the earth, and it is thus his karma to ensure its re-entry when the earth is strong enough to receive it. Moreover the gnomes assemble all their forces for this time, for they see their chief mission in using the moon substance gradually to disperse earth substance into the universe, whilst gathering the most varied experiences to incorporate into the firm structure of Jupiter evolution.

When the moon does unite, all the thoughts of the shadowy intellect which at present have no reality at once become substantial realities. There springs forth a terrible brood of beings, automata lying between the mineral and plant kingdoms, possessed of an overwhelming power of intellect. This swarm spreads over the earth as a ghastly network of spiderlike creatures, all interlocked and imitating in their movements the thoughts of the intellect, interweaving with masterly intelligence but intensely evil intent. Those who have not quickened to life their concepts must live together with this ghastly brood. This is very emphatically part of human evolution, well known to many who try to hold humanity back from spiritual science.[11] We already see its beginnings today in the internet.

The reunion with the moon brings the culmination of evil on earth. The whole Post-Atlantean epoch then ends with the *War of All against All*, caused by the increase of egoism, self-seeking and selfishness. This epoch has on the one hand the task of developing the ego, but this also causes its downfall. The same ego that gives the possibility of independence and inner freedom also causes people to harden themselves within themselves, directing all their wishes to the satisfaction of their own egos, driving away all others and fighting them. It then brings war of each single person against each other person in every branch of life, class against class, sex against sex. Far worse than modern warfare with weapons, this is a conflict of souls, difficult for present consciousness to understand. There are frightful, devastating moral entanglements, and every imaginable subtlety in the use of physical forces. 'You do not know that you are wretched and pitiable and poor and blind and naked' (Rev. 3: 17). Only through selflessness is it possible to preserve mankind from the brink of destruction. And the desolation is that the human being himself bears the blame. 'As many as I love I reprove and discipline, so be zealous and change your ideas' (Rev. 3: 19) (thus those who have not yet turned to the spirit are also loved).

The 'Little Apocalypse' (Mark 13: 14–19) refers to this time in the words: 'Let them that be in Judaea flee to the mountains. And let him that is on the housetop not go down into the house, nor enter to take anything out of his house. And let him that is in the field not turn back again to take up his garment. But woe to them that are with child, and to them that give suck in those days. For in those days shall be affliction such as was not from the beginning of the creation when God created until now, nor shall be again.'

This seventh age is prepared under the influence of

Capricorn, the Goat, characterized by taming the animal forces, and by bending the knee for the upward leap. Its philosophy of Spiritism asserts that only spirit is real.

The time that outlasts the War contains no principle of progress. It is necessary for nation, race, sex, position and differences of religion to be wiped out from human karma. The individual acquires more and more power, but mankind does not thereby become more democratic, and it is impossible to conceive what might occur if selflessness has not been attained – the most brutal forces would lead. This will happen.[12]

Christ's Tiny Band

In this critical time, moral forces still hold sway, the moral sense unfolds, and virtue can be taught and learned. A number of people can now perceive the presence of Christ in the form in which he manifests in Higher Spiritland. After manifesting physically, etherically and astrally, he now comes in all his glory as the most sublime Ego, the spiritualized Ego Self, the mighty teacher of human evolution, the very essence and embodiment of the 'I'. We have seen (p. 55) that progressive mankind now lives in the clouds. 'Like lightning coming forth from the east and flashing into the west will be the presence (*parousia*) of the Son of Man ... They will see the Son of Man coming on the clouds of heaven with power and great glory' (Matt. 24: 27–30). This is *the actual 'second coming'*. 'We shall be caught in the clouds to meet the Lord in the air' (1 Thess. 4: 17).

This, his true 'I', far transcends every human 'I'; and the light in which he now comes gives humanity the highest moral impulses. He evolves as Ego Christ to be the Spirit of the Earth – a process already begun at Golgotha. He then rises to even higher stages with all mankind, a mighty

cosmic Ego that is like a great group-soul of all humanity.[13]
'I am the beauteous shepherd who lays down his soul for
his sheep* ... So there shall be one flock, one shepherd'
(John 10: 11–16).

The Christ impulse now works especially through a third
Eloha as a sort of prophetic nature, since the age must
prepare to pass into an entirely new epoch, and prophecy is
a stimulus to the will. Many of those who spiritualized
themselves in the sixth age are no longer present, for they
are carried over. The certainty of souls who have accepted
the spiritual life that this has not been in vain lies in the
strong force of hope that a new culture which they know
has been prepared spiritually is soon to appear in outer life.
Only exceptional individuals remain on earth to understand fully what the future is to bring, and to experience the
complete reception of Christ into their inner being. There
awaken in them in abundance the forces of love, which can
become the fount for all knowledge, all incentives, all
deeds. As such they are inevitably persecuted by the others
who cannot understand them: 'Blessed are those who are
persecuted for righteousness' sake, for theirs is the kingdom of heaven' (Matt. 5: 10). The virtue of Capricorn is
courage, which becomes power of redemption; and the
corresponding vice — envy — is easily understood.

Those who are most advanced in developing Life Spirit
through the power of thought, as guides to the soul's inner
depths, are the Masters of Wisdom and of the Harmony of
Feelings, namely, Christian Rosencreutz and Jesus of
Nazareth. Only now do even they fully understand Christ,

---

*Editor's note: *kalos* means beauty, rather than good — Christ ascribes
goodness only to the Father (Mark 10: 18). *Psyche* means soul rather than
life. Beauty is the lifting of what is physical to the realm of the divine,
which is precisely what Christ now does; and the giving of his soul as
group-soul of humanity goes beyond the giving of his life on Golgotha.

forming organs of sight. 'And God said, let there be light' (Gen. 1: 3). Organs of warmth, hearing and touch were also formed. Further contraction in the earth-moon produced watery substance, and this flowed in and out of human bodies; these were shaped by sound like a fish in the water below, but above consisted of vapour touched by light. The moon-earth began to rotate slowly, and 'God divided the light from the darkness' (Gen. 1: 4). By night the bodies disintegrated, but by day their fire was refertilized from the universal astrality. Shining plant and animal forms whirled through the ether.

During the Lemurian epoch, which echoed the ancient Moon evolution, hermaphrodite bodies were first developed out of the whole earth-moon organism, and swam in the atmosphere above a watery surface. As the air was breathed into them ('God breathed into his nostrils the breath of life'—Gen. 3: 7) the forms dried out and hardened, so that souls could hold them only briefly; and the solid element appeared. But into the warmth which now circulated within the air like blood, Lucifer also entered, opening eye and ear to the sense world in exchange for knowledge of good and evil—the Fall of Man. All but the strongest souls—represented as Adam— were drawn away to other planets by luciferic spirits, and thus came under luciferic influence. To restore the balance, Jehovah withdrew the moon from the Pacific region, taking with it the strongest hardening forces and sending thence the forces of wisdom to shape humanity for the coming of love. Gradually the earth took on its present shape. Souls were able to return, and as human bodies became upright the sexes divided. Human karma began. These physical bodies were still soft, pliable and transparent, the etheric bodies grotesque and animal-like, even dragonlike below. They remained in the atmosphere, whilst primal plant and animal forms began to touch the solid earth forming below. Lemuria ended in a fire-catastrophe caused by uncontrolled human passions.

The Atlantean (Tertiary) epoch saw the differentiation of humanity into races, souls who had returned from the planets being guided by the corresponding oracles. Human willing was now strong, with magic power especially over the plant forces, and memory reached back through the ancestors. The human physical body, sufficiently condensed to reflect a simple ego-consciousness, should have reverted to a fluid condition. But because of the Fall hardening continued, and the etheric head was drawn down into the physical. Understanding of 'the speech of nature' gave way to human speech. Except for a nucleus who were led to Central Asia, degeneration set in amid the rigours of the Ice Ages and tectonic movements. The epoch ended in the sinking of Atlantis, which resulted from the prolonged misuse of esoteric knowledge.

The whole of the Post-Atlantean epoch should, but for the Fall, have been again on a spiritual level similar to that of Lemuria, with the addition of ego-consciousness.[1] This of course did not happen, but cultures continued on the physical plane until the Mystery of Golgotha brought a new impulse, not only for the involution of civilization back to the spirit but also for the whole future of the world and humanity. Now, instead of three and a half epochs for the process of respiritualization, only two and a half were left (i.e. $17\frac{1}{2}$ ages instead of $24\frac{1}{2}$). Instead of the most significant steps on man's upward path taking place epoch by epoch, they consequently occur later—between the sixth and seventh ages of the present epoch, the fourth and fifth ages of the sixth, and between the second and third ages of the seventh epoch. Hence the completely new conditions in the seventh Post-Atlantean age, with a new form of reproduction, incarnation in the clouds, and the return of the moon. This need to 'catch up' also opened the way for Ahriman, who always aims to rush ahead.

*   *   *

The sixth epoch is more spiritual than the present; human life does not just flow on according to causality on the physical plane, but even outwardly becomes *the expression or manifestation of the astral or soul world*. That world, described by Rudolf Steiner in his *Theosophy*, is not separated from the sense-perceptible world, but is today normally experienced only after death, at the stage called kamaloca. It consists entirely of sympathy and antipathy, pleasure and pain, warmth and cold. The soul then tends to pay attention to its own etheric body, and how this is received by the elemental world, namely, beings similar to itself. By looking at its ever-changing fate it becomes aware of what it has been. Now in the sixth epoch everyone awakens step by step to the cultures of the previous epoch, which are already visible to the initiate, and to what must be done to rectify mistakes. 'Behold, a door opened in heaven ... Come up hither and I will show you things that must occur hereafter' (Rev. 4: 1).

This leads on to the great vision of the throne in heaven surrounded by 24 elders (seven epochs of Saturn, Sun and Moon evolutions plus three on earth before the descent of humanity). In the centre is the Lamb, the sign of the Redeemer, the group soul for the higher manifestation of humanity which will exist as long as will the earth.

Around the throne are four living creatures, which resemble a lion, a bull, one with a human face, and an eagle, each with six wings and eyes inside and out. They depict the principle creative forces flowing from the zodiac, having been the main originators of Saturn, Sun, Moon and Earth evolution respectively. (The eagle first appears as scorpion, but is destined to soar upwards). All four have, however, worked throughout (as distinct from the zodiac forces at single successive stages of evolution), and came over from the Moon as spirit-prototypes of humanity as it developed on earth. We do not disclose the inner nature of our astral body as does an animal, but in reality we all still have within us this common group-soul ego in which these four still manifest; and now that the individual discovers his relation to the Godhead they start to act.

All the Imaginations, Inspirations and Intuitions which we have given out into the world consciously or unconsciously by means of our bones, muscles and nerves respectively, even only since the catastrophe of Atlantis, are still present as part of the environment and must gradually be received again into our souls. And more particularly, the aspects of character not harmonized during the Post-Atlantean cultures, which are still imprinted on the etheric body, now rise in succession in order that we can bring them back into the regular progression of evolution. The creatures in succession recapitulate the specific impulses of these cultures. Rather than feeling oneself the ruler of nature, one here feels oneself as a child of the Hierarchies and a companion of the deceased.

A third of those who began evolution have at this stage attained the goal, a third will only do so later, and a third are falling away. Most people thus have some tendency to evil, but the possibility of turning to good is far stronger.

The return of the moon in the previous age cannot but have an effect on the totality of the earth itself, which consists of nine layers.[2] Evolution thus implies a transformation of the earth's interior. Now if we consider any planet, there is a counter-planet in the interior of the earth which is the mirror, the reversal, of what is outside; and we use what is outside to grasp what is inside. It is, however, only possible to correlate the five traditional planets with the nine layers if account is also taken of the fourfold nature of the moon, as experienced in kamaloca. (The outermost planets are described as foreign guests who do not belong to our evolution.) Clearly the karma arising from the origin and development even of a planet must be worked over in its dispersal. In the absence of any known indication from Rudolf Steiner as to when the planets and interior of the earth are reincorporated into progressive involution, the placing of descriptions that follow in this respect must be regarded as subject to subsequent amendment.

The First Three Ages

Those few individuals who survived on earth the War of All Against All, together with the many spiritually minded individuals who had lifted themselves above it, provide the foundation for a new start. Their inner life, consisting of all they have done, good and bad, which we call 'I', is now inside the whole sphere of the moon envelope. Within the 'I' lives as much of Spirit Self as they have individually been able to receive. They work from the words: 'I am the Res-urrection and the Life' (John 11: 25).

They look down to the earth as an outside world, where their previous thoughts and feelings form clouds and con-stellations, at the centre of which they experience the inner organic nature of mankind as a whole. They speak forth bodies below through the larynx, using them from above as instruments. Our present body is a temple in which the Hierarchies are at work, and to construct out of the larynx bodies that operate effectively requires insight into the way in which they live, create and work through the human 'I'. The results are of course quite different from bodies today — the heart, for instance, is a voluntary organ, and today's higher astral senses become sense organs. Six thousand years from today the ideas of present natural science no longer hold good; but new nature forces are available, transformed from the moral realities of previous ages.

Those who have ennobled their inner life and attained wisdom and spirituality not only show this on their forehead and in their whole physiognomy, but express it in their gestures — indeed the whole body is now an image of the soul. Progressive people have radiant, good features and noble benevolent expressions; those who were lukewarm or turned away, preserving backward forces and retarding evolution, reveal their evil passions and impulses hostile to the spirit in ugly, unintelligent, evil-looking countenances and corresponding gestures, which they cannot hide. *Mankind is thus visibly divided into two great streams, the good and the evil.*

The first task for this age must be to master the initial interaction between the moon and the earth, and especially to control the spiderlike network of intellectual automata (p. 59). The first impulse from the moon is known as 'glowing desires', arising from the lower instinctive nature for things of the sense world, which form the solid element of the elementary world. Antipathy here predominates over sympathy, bringing about separation and egoism. These desires meet the brittle mineral layer of the earth's surface, only a few miles thick, which is likewise characterized by the hard outlines of the mineral world separated in space.

To bring this into order it is necessary for the great majority of people to learn to live actively in a structure of pure sense-free *thoughts*, free from desires, in which one thought grows out of another as in mathematics. This is the Rosicrucian stage of 'study'. When such thinking extends to the whole content of spiritual science, the stupendous facts of evolution and of the spiritual world stimulate the feelings to resound to such an extent that they predominate over all that is merely intellectual.

This age is prepared and carried by impulses from the realm of Sagittarius, the Archer, shooting down from the cosmos. Its virtue is appropriately Control of the Tongue, which becomes Feeling for Truth. Its gesture is resolve (thought that seeks to make itself felt in reality), whilst its philosophy of Monism recognizes many beings with varied powers.

The Apocalypse represents this age (Rev. 6: 2) by the first creature, the lion, namely, the powerful people whose heart forces and feelings have been strengthened, calling forth a white horse. White, the soul image of the spirit, recalls the purity of the ancient Indian culture, when people were still inspired by beings from the planetary spheres and had as yet no desires for the newly perceptible physical world. The animal form of the horse indicates those who still wish to remain unchanged from the pre-Christian cultures when Lucifer properly separated people from the original common group-soul by developing egoism. The 'I' as rider now carries a bow—the cosmic forces of the Archer—representing the above-mentioned power of creative thought added by Christianity. As the rider comes forth 'overcoming and to overcome' the desires of the senses, he is given a crown, an aura, representing the redemption of the head forces of knowledge—perception, thinking and memory.

As people thus lose their desires for the sense world, the original influence of Lucifer is averted, and there is a period of selfhood without its evils. Moreover Christ, who approaches as an Angel-like being, enters the power of memory, extending it so that the whole of earthly evolution can now be surveyed. But where he is not received, memory becomes chaotic and people get duller and duller, which is nothing but a fall into the Abyss.

*   *   *

The second region of the soul world and of the moon sphere is an ever-changing mood of 'fleeting susceptibility' where rigid brain-bound thinking and the glitter of life unworthy of humanity have finally to be cast aside. But the ever-changing quality of the mood enables it to grasp in feeling the ever-changing fluid aspect of the elementary world that is the basis of life on earth.

The layer below the earth's surface is similarly half liquid and relatively soft, and is known as the Fluid Earth. It has no actual life, but contains the forces through which any life is immediately expelled and destroyed. It is thus truly a sphere of death, which gives rise to the lifeless inorganic mineral kingdom out of the living world — for everything dead derives from the living, not vice versa. Moreover it degrades the living thought world to our dead, abstract intellectual concepts. It is held under tremendous pressure by the mineral layer, and if released would instantaneously explode into cosmic space. It has its own dull consciousness like certain kinds of plants. It can be perceived at the stage of Scourging, which bears calmly every suffering and hindrance, equivalent to pure concentration. It was during Atlantis that the mineral kingdom, hitherto still living and malleable, became hard and dead; and the karma of this has now to be dissolved through the life-forces of the rhythmic system.

This is possible because the second age is prepared and guided from the region of the Scorpion, the character of which is to take into oneself a poisonous sting that one must resist. The moral aspect of this is the rise of *feelings* preparing a different relation to evil than confrontation, namely, to take it in and transform it within oneself. Steiner's Scorpio verse refers to 'expiatory self-building' and 'corrective world-wielding'. And the virtue of Scorpio — patience that becomes insight — is essential if one is actually to 'turn the other cheek' etc. (Matt. 5: 39). A quite different morality thus begins to unfold, just as in kamaloca relationships are experienced from the aspect of the other person. Only in this Christian way can evil arising from the earth be overcome without creating new karma: 'I am the way, the truth and the life' (John 14: 6). But Scorpio's gesture of cleverness still contains the danger of pride.

This dual aspect of the Scorpion—the sting of death and its healing—also makes possible the redemption of all that is still untransformed from the second Persian age, when Zarathustra proclaimed the great Sun Being, Ahura Mazda, in his battle with Ahriman and the forces of evil within the earth—what one then acquired still modifies one's countenance now.

In the Apocalypse this age is expressed by the second creature, the bull, which represents the metabolic process and peaceful work, calling forth a red horse (Rev. 6: 4). Red, the living image of the soul, is also aggressive. The rider, who brings the fruits of the ego, is given a sword, and power to take peace from the earth, that people should 'slay' one another, which sounds equally aggressive. But it reflects the quality of the Fluid Earth, and must be transformed to the mystery sense of lifting one another from the earthly to the spirit, rather than neglecting through sloth or superficiality the way to the divine. Thereby the Scorpion becomes the Eagle, neutralizing the impulse of death and awakening new life. The earth itself tends to wake up again; with the neutralizing of the Fluid Earth; the inorganic minerals again become living.

* * *

By the third age the earth is once more awake, active, living and plantlike; the dense quartzes have again become fluid, the whole primeval Alpine range has dissolved, and

people and animals are again malleable, as they were in the
fifth Atlantean age, but with everything that they have
meanwhile earned.[3]

The third region of the moon sphere is that of 'wish
substance', in which feelings of sympathy predominate,
attracting everything around them, although with an
underlying tone of selfishness. This is the airy aspect of the
elemental world—airy wishes—which supports the astral
body.

The third layer within the earth is the Vapour Earth (Air
Earth or Sensitivity Stratum), like a watery vapour with life
present at every point. It is will-like, permeated in a material sense with forces similar to human and animal
passions and impulses. But here feelings are annulled from
the ensouled reality to give rise to the plant kingdom, rather
as the second layer extinguished life. It is thus a circle of
inverted consciousness, which reacts to feelings of living
beings and converts pleasure into pain and vice versa. It too
has an enormous force of expansion, only with effort held
fast hitherto by the mineral layer. It can be perceived by the
capacity of 'Crowning with Thorns'. When people spiritually overcome pain through serenity, they overcome this
layer. The plant kingdom was separated off in late Lemuria,
and this karma must now be overcome.

This age is prepared and guided by Libra, the Scales,
whose gesture is to enter the inorganic world seeking balance. The purified astral body now receives everything
coming to it weighed in thought with a just balance. The
philosophy of Libra is Realism, and since everyone can now
hear speaking within themselves those with whom they are
karmically connected, everything in reality is directed to
balancing karma in the realm of the *will*.

The third creature, with the human face (Rev. 6: 5), which
expresses justice and the predominance of the astral body,
calls forth a black horse (black is the spiritual image of

death). The ego as rider holds the Scales, and a voice is heard putting a price on work and grain, while keeping from harm the fluids that underlie life. The Egypto-Chaldean age reappears here, when measurement, weighing and calculating were introduced, all in fact annulling a purely feeling element.

There are also present now some who practise evil quite consciously, aided by highly developed intellects but lacking feelings — Realism may also bring decay and mineralization of the inner life. Hence it is necessary for sufficient souls to become strong enough to protect the good from the evil ones by a spiritual alchemy; and there are indeed those who can use occult forces to transform the evil ones quite radically into good.[4] This has to be done, not through strife — another evil — but through feelings of mildness, kindness, charitableness, through entering into the evil ones to redeem them. It is the path of the Lamb, the washing of the feet (John 13: 5), offering one's cloak also.

But there has to be a special community in which such an impulse of will can flow, appealing to the best forces from below. The Manichaean Order,* outwardly exterminated long ago by the established religions but inwardly unbroken, has long been training its members for this task, especially by emphasizing purity in the outer life. It now develops from a very small flame to a mighty spiritual fire. Much obduracy and hardness is needed to close the heart and mind to its powerful impressions. Taking on consciously the adverse karma of another in exchange for one's own (p. 44) here plays a special role, without which the earth could not reach its goal.

Through having to make supreme esoteric efforts of will to rescue the evil, good itself receives the greatest strengthening; those concerned gain a quite special good-

---

*See the editor's book: *Mani, His Life and Work.*

ness, a condition of moral holiness which comes only from the realm of the Father.[5] This is hinted at in Christ's words: 'I am the true vine, and my Father is the husbandman' (John 15: 1). This points to the last of the six Eloha-powers brought to earth by Christ (p. 38); he is now present on earth in the fullness of his power.

The Fourth Age

The fourth level of kamaloca now unsealed is the illusion of selfhood based on strength of feeling, on likes and dis-likes — the very stuff of karmic relationships. Karma is finally balanced in the good stream, for whom work that has been in progress ever since Lemuria is brought to a certain conclusion: *Karma comes to an end.*[6]

Participation in a common soul world means losing the feeling of bodily self on which the lower ego is based, and awareness of being even bodily hollowed out. The 'I' acquired in the fourth age of our epoch is united with the entire outer world, whilst the physical body is seen in its true aspect as a body of organizing forces, devoid of sub-stances. 'Resurrection of the body' thus acquires its mean-ing. Every progressive individual thus ascends to the free ether as an immortal spirit free from death,[7] for Christ has indeed conquered death. This is the *laying aside of the last physical body*, also known as the 'first death'.

When the bony system crumbles away, Imaginations remain; when the muscles decay, Inspirations; and when nerves decay, Intuitions remain. These are constituents of the astral and etheric bodies, and continue to live as soul and spirit of the whole earth until carried over to Jupiter existence. Moreover Christ has formed his own astral body out of human wonder, trust and reverence, his etheric body out of compassion and love, and the

equivalent of his physical body out of human conscience. But these capacities depend on a body of flesh,
and must by now be completed. Any wrongs or short-
comings have deprived him of full development, and
leave Earth evolution imperfect.[8] Moreover the last petal
of memory in the 16-petal lotus flower is completed,
and this organ 'revolves like a whirlwind', so that whatever one utters works directly into the astral body of
the other person. Thus the command to love one
another (John 15: 12) takes on quite special significance.

The forces of Virgo, the Virgin, which prepare and guide
this age, stand at the threshold of light and dark, life and
death, with a gesture of soberness bringing about maturity
and dissolving of form. The philosophy of Virgo is
Phenominalism, taking the world just as it appears, which
is now the etheric world, since the majority have from now
on no physical body, no spatial body, only a time body. It is
a real threshold (p. 66).

The Graeco-Latin age here appears again, when art conquered the beauty of the physical at the expense of the
spiritual world becoming dark, whereas now the spiritual is
established at the expense of the physical. The etheric
reflects what was achieved in Greece, and since the Greeks
reflected Atlantean culture, aspects of that are also resurrected.

The Apocalypse depicts the fourth creature—the eagle,
representing a strong 'I' and an enhanced power of religious enthusiasm—as calling forth a pale green horse
signifying the dying lower nature (green is the dead image
of life). 'And his name who sat on it was Death, and Hades
followed him. And authority was given them to kill the
fourth (physical) part of the earth' (Rev. 6: 8). Thus the
emergence of the Fluid Earth, the source of death in nature,
and the Sensitivity Earth, source of annulment of feelings,
culminate at this stage; for Hades is the realm of soul-

destruction (Matt. 10: 28). From now on all is living and ensouled.

The spiritual leadership of humanity now passes for the first time from a higher being to a human Manu (one who has fully developed Spirit Self); but this must be purchased by his taking all suffering upon himself. One characteristic of Virgo is complete isolation; humanity is now on its own. The virtue of Virgo is courtesy that becomes heart tact, namely, a continuation of the mildness and love of the last age.

There are however still some who wish to remain in the pre-Christian cultures of Lucifer, or are tormented by desires for the material to which they have chained themselves. They fall back on the physical moon-earth, which is at the peak of a new ice age, rigidifying the abandoned physical relics.

The Last Three Ages

The fifth region of the soul world is that of Soul Light, the realm of Mercury, where souls develop sympathy for their soul-surroundings, and let themselves be shone upon by other beings, not for their own sakes but for the others. Progressive souls are continually present, since there is no death, only transformation; and they are inwardly awakened and filled with the light of Christ. The lower soul has been stifled, its impurities done away with, and hence the 'I' appears clothed in innocence. This 'I', which consists of its deeds, not what it thinks itself to 'be' or 'know', circles outside the moon envelope. But instead of being able to see this from without, it retains the memory of a vision on the inner wall resulting from earlier incarnations on earth. The immortality of this 'I' purified by Christ, the spiritualized intelligence, shines forth into the remaining airy warmth of earth.

This fifth age is prepared and guided by the forces of Leo, the Lion, through which active inner organs such as the (etheric) heart and lung which are adapted to their surroundings are filled out and surged through with sunny radiance and enthusiasm. The virtue of compassion here becomes freedom.

The Apocalypse no longer speaks of a horse, for mere intellectual thought no longer exists. Instead, 'I saw beneath the altar the souls of those slain for God's Word and for the witness they bore' (Rev. 6: 9), who were given a white robe and told to wait until their number was completed. Nothing new arises from within the earth at this stage.

Amid our fifth Anglo-Germanic age which now reappears are some individuals—especially in the Rosicrucian-anthroposophical stream—whose astral bodies are already illuminated and permeated by the light of the true 'I', and these are now normally the first to have the spiritual world around them. Those put to death for the sake of the Word at the end of our age (p. 40), who suffer much, are the most important cultural force.

Near the end of this age another great Cosmic New Year is reached after a further 12,000 years. Only now does true Christianity come to expression in outer forms that resemble Christ Jesus; for the creative thought embodied in Christians hitherto has only been the first Christianity, transitory like the rest of creation. The task of humanity during this whole sixth epoch is to establish Life Spirit (the transformation of the etheric body, the realm of the elements) to the extent possible on earth, just as the fifth epoch established Spirit Self in the consciousness soul. This can only be achieved when the good are able to lead those who are evil back to good.

Now, however, Christ brings life to the spirit itself, *creating Life Spirit* in those who have been passed by and 'slain' (i.e. freed from the body). We may call the meeting with Life Spirit (which today can occur every Christmas time) the meeting with Christ in the very depths of the soul. Life Spirit and Christ are the same stream, seen spiritually.[9] Thus the inner Word rises again, in that the spirit now enables it to resound within through Inspiration. Thereby religion receives new dignity.

The evil race with its savage impulses, dominated by the philosophy of Leo that sensations alone are real, now dwells in unchanged animal forms indicated symbolically by the Sphinx. And when those chosen by Christ describe their situation, there sound forth in the Abyss names of blasphemy from the unredeemed who still seek to escape from what they see as spiritual transformation.

* * *

By the sixth age those who prepared for the eternal in the pre-Christian mysteries and have since transformed themselves through the Christ impulse form a great multitude, permeated by the eternal spiritual world. They now work from the periphery in the realm of the invisible.[10] Across the Threshold the sun indeed appears as black and the moon a dull red (Rev. 6: 12). People 'break the eggshell' of the vault of heaven, so that the whole of Spiritland spreads out before them: 'The sky departed, as a scroll is rolled up' (Rev. 6: 14). Instead of sun, moon and stars being studied spatially, their forces are now experienced within the soul; as we know them, the stars have indeed 'fallen to earth'.

It is the Russian age that now appears again, when brotherhood was first developed on the basis of peripheral consciousness (p. 45). But the Russian age was also thoroughly permeated with technology; it poisoned the air, the physical basis of astrality, so that now when feelings are carried into the air they change the whole of nature, and something like a meteor shower occurs. Russian electromagnetic effects similarly work back to cause earthquakes, which release further forces of nature, namely, the Form Earth.

The Form Earth (Soul Earth, Water Earth) was formed before the moon left the earth in Lemuria, and is still in an astral condition. It is the primary source of all outer things on earth, mineral, plant, animal and human — everything in the three layers above — and also contains the archetypal forces which condense into the physical. It is a whirlwind of forms, but a negative picture — the forms of things are as it were changed into their opposites, like a seal and its imprint. All a thing's qualities pass out into its surroundings and spread all around like a plaster cast enclosing an empty space. 'All men, slave or free, hid themselves in caves and in the rocks of the mountains' (Rev. 6: 15).

The Form Earth, which can be grasped by the faculty of 'Carrying the Cross' (feeling the body as a foreign object), thus produces in the material realm the effects that occur spiritually in the first region of spiritland, and prepares for the transition to the next epoch. The age is prepared and guided by the forces of Cancer, the Crab, which work to enclose inner being from the external world.

But Cancer also leads to initiative and action. The sixth region of the soul world is known as Active Soul Force, the realm of Venus, where even scientific and artistic work for its own sake (which still relate to the physical world) must be set aside in favour of a free outpouring of soul forces.

Thus in this sixth age of the sixth epoch comes the first intimate decision for souls. The multitude robed in white, who have now worked over the entire astral body, and retain it, receive the seal of God on their foreheads (Rev. 7: 1-17). But those who still follow the Cancer philosophy of materialism, weighted in matter, must suffer the great day of vengeance and the ordeal (Rev. 6: 12-17), and are drawn down by the Angel of the Abyss.

* * *

The seventh region of the soul world to descend is known as Soul Life, the sun sphere. Here souls are freed from any last remains of inclination towards bodily life, and manifest in free outpouring and absorption into the spirit. The spiritual aspect of the sun becomes experience. The 'I' now knows that it was a sun-being before the Fall, to which it must again progress. Freed from everything connected with personality and completely worked into the astral body, it no longer needs the support of angelic forces, and develops a religious life suited to all humanity. By the end of the sixth epoch Spirit Man is incorporated into humanity through an impulse coming from the Father.

This seventh age is prepared and guided by the forces of Gemini, the Twins; the two groups of humanity are separate. The quality of Gemini lies behind the light in and beyond the zodiac, and its gesture is one of harmony and mobility, fusing duality into unity on the basis of the ego. Its virtue is perseverance that becomes faithfulness.

The American age that now reappears created nothing new of spiritual value; nevertheless Christ then appeared in the fullness of his Cosmic Ego. Now he is felt not only mystically but known in Inspiration through spiritual sound; and the inner nature of the Word can be further perceived through Intuition.[11] Here the soul also becomes intimately acquainted with Lucifer, the light spirit.

The evildoers are in the Abyss. Hence the Apocalypse speaks of 'silence in heaven' (Rev. 8: 1). The ending of the whole sixth epoch is indicated by the throwing down to earth of the golden censer filled from the altar fire (Rev. 8: 5). The inner nature of the sun becomes earth experience.

6

The Seventh Epoch (Trumpets)

The First Four Ages

This epoch completes the physical condition of form of the earth, which must then be entirely transmuted into astral form. But only in human beings is matter annihilated. So it must all be absorbed by us — we must not despise matter, but unite with it. Lemuria, when matter first solidified, is thus redeemed.

Steiner does not describe the seven ages separately, but he does indicate that this epoch must be regarded as the *earthly expression of Spiritland*, which now descends to earthly manifestation. The seven stages of Spiritland are described in his book *Theosophy*. The characteristic experience there after death is that the astral body gets larger, looser and thinner, so that as it is absorbed into the spirit the past is lost — a real forgetting — but it returns later in an altered manner, showing what it must become in future. In terms of involution this must mean the spiritualization of the elementary world, which is the outer manifestation of the astral world, to reappear at the periphery in the next Condition of Life (p. 105). The ego must penetrate from the astral to the etheric by means of Inspiration to hear the spiritual sounds expressed in the Apocalypse as the seven trumpets.

Everything now enters consciousness from within (like memory), not from without. It is all ordered according to measure and number, the music of the spheres. And spirit beings impel the 'I' to represent their influence in colours and sounds. Every thought rings forth outwardly, so nothing can be hidden in any way, for thinking is part of the world process itself.

*   *   *

The first region of Lower Spiritland, the 'continental', contains the archetypes* out of which all inorganic substances, including our physical corporality, were created. It shaped them as hollow spaces — nothings — from outside, in colours complementary to the physical. Whatever we do to this mineral kingdom, either in industry or in art, by means of 'the plough of the spirit' passes into the very atoms. By now every single atom will have been worked over. The silent, unpretentious, passionless nature of the stone possesses an extraordinary magical force, which progressive people thus attain.

This realm also contains the outward forms of our various incarnations and the basic power of love between blood relations and friends. A certain degree of self-knowledge is needed to draw from the cosmic life beyond the solar system the forces (such as those of Christ) that are necessary to liberate oneself from the inorganic in order to progress further.

At the sound of the first trumpet, hail and fire mixed with blood are hurled to earth; a third part of the earth, with trees and grass, is burnt up (Rev. 8: 7).

*   *   *

The second region of Spiritland is the 'oceanic', where archetypes of everything living, the creative forces of the etheric sea, form a common life of wisdom that streams through the world like its blood. Thinking transforms *all substance* into something living, which is absorbed by the human being and *passes into nothingness*; mere pictures of it would remain, were it not that new forces brought through

---

* Archetypes are spiritual beings of various levels, ceaselessly creating, who manifest as living thoughts independent of the human being.

the Mystery of Golgotha give them a new reality as picture-
warmth, a quite new substance.[1] This region also contains
the bond of love formed in a group through religious life or
common reverence for the unit and harmony of the universe, and the 'I' becomes one with all that lives in and
through the zodiac.

At the sounding of the second trumpet a blazing mountain is hurled into the sea, a third of the sea is changed to
blood, and a third of its creatures die (Rev. 8: 9).

*   *   *

Third is the 'atmospheric' region, which contains the
flowing archetypes that form and organize the astral qualities of all beings into a common world: sensations,
pains and sorrows, joys, passions, longings, instincts
and feelings. It also contains deeds of love and devotion that bear fruit in service of the wider community. Human egos look down from the sun sphere and
speak formatively, creatively, into the warmth substance, calling forth beings such as existed in ancient
Saturn or the Polarean epoch. Any coarser elements that
remain are in chaotic condition, attached to the finer
parts like cast-off skins or shells.

At the third trumpet the flaming star called Wormwood
falls on a third of the rivers, its bitterness bringing death to
many people (Rev. 8: 10).

*   *   *

The fourth region, pure Spiritland, is an etheric sphere
containing as thoughts the archetypes of human deeds
performed out of love for humanity as a whole, whether
artistic, scientific or statesmanlike — one witholds the means
to radiate outwards, and consciously becomes one with the

whole community. It controls the ordering and grouping of the lower regions.

Since the laws of entropy are fully justified, the physical earth will indeed end through a kind of heat death. The more the soul is warmed by the powers of love gained through the Christ impulse, the more powerfully can it astralize matter. Now begins the transformation through feelings of the last element, the warmth which underlies the human 'I'. The picture-warmth that results in our feelings is in fact what the Christ substance, the Christ impulse, is.[2] Then this Christ impulse, although a personal matter for every individual, becomes through its very nature the same for all (whereas the intelligence due to Lucifer is impersonal but divisive). As a collection of cells forms a single being, so brotherhoods evolve into a single essence of humanity.

We are consequently concerned here with the end of ordinary ego-consciousness (which is based on warmth). Instead we enter a realm of mental pictures, which are either raised to life-filled imaginations or revert in the Abyss to the stage of the Old Moon; and *one dimension of space ('a third part') is replaced by that of time*.

At the fourth trumpet a third part of sun, moon and stars is darkened, ending a third part of day and of night (Rev. 8: 12).

*   *   *

All these four regions of Spiritland are thus transformed from above, from the spirit, not from within the earth. Life is withdrawn progressively from plants, animals and human beings through the gate of warmth, and the cosmos loses its light. Tone, not light, now rules completely.

It was during the time between the separation of the sun and that of the moon from the earth that the inner planets, Mercury and Venus, were originally separated from the sun, as domiciles for luciferic Spirits of Form who could not keep up with the pace of the sun. Rudolf Steiner is not recorded as speaking of when or how they reunite, but it is conceivable that they might first reunite with the earth, now etheric, as 'the fiery mountain' and 'the star Wormwood'.

The Fifth and Sixth Ages

The fifth region marks the transition to the influences of Higher Spiritland, the descended realm of intentions and aims which form the archetypes of all lower regions. Spirit Self (p. 47) is here developed to a high degree, such that one repeats again and again the words of Paul: 'Not I, but Christ in me does everything' — thus does one live. One is fully oneself, able to work freely amid memories of previous lives and prophetic visions of the future, and in the presence of all the exalted beings before whom the divine wisdom is outspread, who pour this wisdom into their environment, revealing its significance. This enables one to make the ennobled etheric into a new being which can live in the coming astralized state. Spirit Self appears in the Apocalypse as 'a star fallen from heaven to earth, to which was given the key to the shaft of the Abyss' (Rev. 9: 1). What is this shaft?

The next layer of the earth, formed between the exit of sun and moon, is called the Fruit Earth (Seed Earth, Fertility Earth) and is the source of all terrestrial life. Even as material it teems with exuberant energy, rampant fertility, every little part perpetually emitting new impulses; form after form arises from it and passes away. This life serves the layers above that hold it in place, and has the capacities of a soul striving for formation. It can be perceived at the stage of Mystical Death (facing nothingness, the rending of the veil and descent into hell — the first real knowledge of what evil is). Moreover this Fruit Earth is connected by a sort of channel to a hollow space in the uppermost layer, through which work its forces and those from below it—a real 'shaft' of the Abyss. Here the Apocalypse depicts a cloud of locusts (which can breed with great rapidity and destroy all vegetation, as excessive life destroys consciousness). Their king, named the Destroyer, is the Angel of the Abyss. They appear like horses, with human faces, lions' teeth and tails like scorpions, which sting but do not kill. They may harm for five months (in this fifth period) only people who lack on their brow the seal of God (p. 81), so that they long to die, but cannot (Rev. 9: 2–11). This is the 'first woe'.

*   *   *

The sixth realm of Spiritland is that of Life Spirit, the transformed etheric, now developed to the highest degree possible on earth, and the seed for what Paul called 'the incorruptible body' (1 Cor. 15: 42). Here the archetypes of life are living germ-points, and the true being of the world and the right course of the world order are established.

But the 'second woe' begins with the release of 'four Angels bound at the River Euphrates' (Rev. 9: 14), the four astral group-souls (bull, lion, human and eagle) that remain untransformed. Following them are 200 million troops of cavalry (those still committed to the intellect) characterized by lions' heads, red, blue and yellow breastplates and serpent tails (depicting the lower soul elements of thinking, willing, feeling and ego respectively). They are authorized to kill a third part of mankind—Christianity kills the lower transitory nature of souls insufficiently ennobled to enter the future astral earth—by means of the fire, smoke and sulphur that comes from their mouths.

This fire comes from the Fire Earth, the foundation of the strata above, into which the primordial fire (of which

mineral fire is mere extract) has been banished. Its substance is pure will, elemental vital force, shot through by
instincts, impulses and passions, joy and pain. It can sense
desire and suffering, and when human sufferings increase
it grows restive; if put under pressure it would cry out. This
stratum is the centre from which Ahriman operates in a
material sense, though here he is in a sense already
shackled. If evil will-impulses work in conjunction, the
shattering effects work up through the shaft to the surface
as earthquakes and volcanic eruptions — such was the
destruction of Lemuria. If morality increases, the tremors
become less severe. The Fire Earth can be perceived at the
stage of 'Burial' (feeling the whole earth as one's body), and
when people have trained their breathing so that it pro-
motes and radiates life, they will overcome it. One may
suppose that the Active Soul Force associated with the
reunited Venus may be particularly crucial here.

This sixth trumpet sounds the experience of '66', when
those who still exercise a high degree of evil, hardened in
matter and unfit for the astral earth, have to form a material
sphere which now separates from the astralizing etheric
earth as a slag, but is not yet ejected. They still have etheric
bodies adapted only to the physical world, and feel fires of
desire for physical sensuality which can no longer be
appeased. What remains of their incarnations stands like a
mighty tableau, scattered and bound to parts of the earth
that remain dead. Their souls are separated in an egoistic
sense, the booty of Lucifer, unable to approach the bodies.[3]
Their etheric bodies are therefore of necessity torn out of
them, and the experience of this is known as 'the second
death'. Those exceptional cases who have taken all 16 paths
which unite too fully with their race — two more in the ages
of our epoch, seven in the sixth and seven in the seventh
epoch — will have a bodiless existence until they appear in
the second half of Jupiter as nature spirits.

The Apocalypse then presents great positive pictures, starting with the mighty Angel wrapped in cloud, his face shining like a sun, his legs as pillars of fire, his right foot on the sea and his left on land (Rev. 10: 1). Progressive people become one with the universal forces of the earth, their heads with the sun forces; their wisdom has become life in the watery etheric and their wills have become strength on land—they are carried by the red and blue bloodstreams. Thus they are represented in cosmic instead of human form.

When the 'seven thunders' speak, the Apocalyptist is mysteriously told not to report it (Rev. 10: 3). This may refer to the deeds of the Hierarchies in the respiritualization of the earth, on which Steiner too remains silent compared with his descriptions of past evolution, or to the rumblings of the layers within the earth already under consideration here.

Thirdly the sun Angel proclaims that '*time (chronos) shall no longer be*' (Rev. 10: 7). This translation is usually changed because it is thought to be incomprehensible. But it is essential, because the Time Beings (Archai) have completed their earthly task. In the imminent astral stage the sequence of events is reversed, the effect coming before the cause, just as when after death one looks back on life.

Fourthly the Angel presents a scroll which is to be eaten, bringing bliss to the soul but bitterness to the body (Rev. 10: 9): the whole power of love contained in the Gospels must be devoured by the soul so that one becomes an embodiment of wisdom and love, but one cannot avoid being 'crucified in the body'.

The End of the Physical/Etheric Earth

The seventh stage of Spiritland is Spirit Man, the true life-kernel which has its origin in still higher realms. With this the problems of body, soul and spirit are solved so far as possible on earth.

People now have a great chunk of the macrocosm within them, worked through in earthly images, and the effects of this transformed astral body first need also to be imprinted on their etheric. The aim is for the experiences of the different cultures to bear fruit for every individual, regardless of their individual destiny. The ether body is an image of the work done consciously, and if this has been done in a Christlike way the body enters worthily into the astral condition; for the conviction that 'Not I but Christ in me does everything' ennobles the etheric into a body of love that can live in the astral world. What individuals have done they keep as a temple in which are to live the new human beings of Jupiter.

Thus those whose etheric bodies come to harmonize completely with the astral now lay them aside without pain—they feel the need to do so, and feel able to build them again if necessary through the forces of Christ. Thus the temple of the soul itself is to be measured as to its fitness for the astral stage, but the outer court, the physical and etheric bodies, are no longer of account (Rev. 11: 1). All those who express what is good, beautiful and noble, who bear an expression of Christ on their countenance, whose words ring out as resounding thoughts that manifest him, are completely spiritualized in the astral cosmic sphere. Their delicate spiritualized bodies become a joyful expression of love in their inmost being; they grow ever more Christlike, irradiating the whole heart with love.

The earth too is completely transformed through Wisdom (science), Beauty (art) and inner Strength, and attains the astral condition—even today it is already getting smaller. It's matter will be dissolved into cosmic space as cosmic dust. Physical laws now coincide with moral laws. But whereas the planets are stars which the gods have already abandoned, Christ leaves no such physical star at the death of the earth. 'The kingdom of the world became that of our Lord and of his Christ, and he shall reign unto the ages of the ages' (Rev. 11: 15).

The period until this takes place—of the order of 40,000 years—is very short compared to the millions or milliards of years reached by the correct but unreal calculations of natural science, which cannot take account of the actions of spiritual beings in the process.[4]

Earth evolution has taken place according to a spiritual plan, the inner structure of which is reformed within humanity under the direction of the Masters of the White Lodge (such as Buddha, Jesus of Nazareth, Christian Rosencreutz). This is compressed to an ever smaller kernel, so that a small copy of the whole physical evolution is carried through the subsequent stages of form, multiplied in Spiritland, and becomes the atoms of the next Condition of Life.

Editor's Note

The descriptions that follow become increasingly difficult for ordinary consciousness to grasp, because they are so different from anything we experience today. Only a living, imaginative thinking thoroughly imbued with the ideas expressed in, for example, Rudolf Steiner's book *An Outline of Occult Science*, which can integrate them into the overall world-conception of anthroposophy, is likely to find them fruitful material for meditation.

7
Stages of Form

The Perfected Astral Stage

As already mentioned, everything that takes form first arises as an archetype in Higher Spiritland, is developed in Lower Spiritland, and takes shape in the astral world before becoming physical. It subsequently returns perfected through the astral world to the transformed intellectual stage of Lower Spiritland and thence to the archetypal stage of Higher Spiritland. Between each stage, for example between the physical stage just completed and the coming astral stage, there is a short *pralaya* or period of inwardization which can be known by Inspiration, and a somewhat sharp transition to new conditions.

All our earthly actions are thus accompanied by astral beings, leaving a trail behind us; the astral stage of form is therefore already prepared. Although personal karma has already been balanced (p. 76), any karmic effects we produced objectively as grotesque astral beings must still be adjusted. This world now appears pictorially to Imagination. The fruits of all we have done in the mineral kingdom unfold again as astral forms — a cathedral, for instance, was once a conception in the 'I' of its architect, and now he produces it again in astral form and endues it with life through his Life Spirit.[1]

We can again shape our astral form from within outwards, shaping at will, for example, an astral hand, as in Atlantis. Through the love that has flowed into humanity, the spiritual soul of the heart streams outwards, surrounding others with deepest feelings; one's soul lies open before them. When one can encounter the whole world in this way, a new organ of perception is ready.[2] Paul calls the etheric body after it has become astral the 'spiritual body' (1 Cor. 15: 40); the 'last Adam' that inhabits it is the inner capacity of Christ.

The 'I' is now so completely worked back into the astral body that it can live at the same tempo as the sun. Those human beings who live in the astral world accordingly draw out the finer part of the earth and unite it with the sun, becoming sun beings, whilst the coarser part remains with the moon. When humanity is sufficiently spiritualized through the Christ forces, the sun spirits who descended to earth at Golgotha bring evolution to the point where the *reunion of sun and earth*, both in astral form, becomes possible.[3] 'God's temple in heaven was laid open' (Rev. 11: 19).

The outcome is depicted by the scene in heaven of the woman clothed with the sun, crowned with twelve stars, who has the moon beneath her feet (Rev. 12: 1). Moon forces that counteract the speed of the sun are no longer needed. She is confronted by a great red dragon, which tries to devour the male child to whom she gives birth; but it is prevented, and she flees to the wilds (Rev. 12: 6).

The earth itself while in astral condition passes spatially through Mercury, which is itself still etheric.

At this point the Apocalypse expresses the reversed time of the astral world by reversing the next group of events, but correlation in the rest of this chapter should be regarded as tentative.

God's vengeance on 'the whore of Babylon', the source of immorality, is depicted at length (Rev. 16: 19–18: 24). She is depicted as riding a scarlet beast, the red dragon again, the snake that appears in heaven. This represents the luciferic forces of the four animal group-souls—lion, bull, human and eagle—that rightly formed mankind in early Atlantis (for higher animal forms are nothing but thoughts and passions woven into bodies when still soft). With three more group-souls from the three later Atlantean ages, these forces appear etherically as seven 'heads'; the corresponding physical forms, the last three duplicated as male and female, are signified as ten 'horns'. These are still present in everyone astrally to the extent that they have not been personally redeemed.

The whore represents all those whose passions and emotions, under the spell of Lucifer, remain uncontrolled, those whose feeling and heart sphere are impoverished; and those involved atavistically in mediumistic clairvoyance, where ego and astral are withdrawn and liable on return to corruption.[4] She is finally consumed in fire by 'the ten horns and the beast' (Rev. 17: 16). The bodies of her followers must be given up as lost, but their egos and astral bodies continue into the evil sub-astral world connected with the moon. 'And the beast that was and is not, he is an eighth, and yet is one of the seven, and goes to destruction' (Rev. 17: 11). They unite with the worst substances of the lower realms in the sub-physical astral world, in an already existing 'eighth sphere'. This consists of astral substance snatched from the Old Moon by Lucifer and Ahriman when the Spirits of Form were forming the Earth, and is now outwith the 'seven stars'. It forms an illegitimate moon ruled by Lucifer, with which those who amass only what serves themselves, or who transform their free will back to visionary clairvoyance, already connect themselves.[5]

In the Perfected Astral stage of Form, seven stages equivalent to epochs are depicted only negatively, as the outpouring of 'the last plagues of all' from the seven bowls of wrath of God (Rev. 15–16). Six broadly resemble those of the Trumpets, for they are still a revelation of divine love, but sullied here by human illusion. Those cast down must experience the counterpart of that which carries the good beings upwards. But when the seventh Angel pours his bowl on the air (astral world), this culminates in 'a violent earthquake like none before it' (Rev. 16: 18).

We must consider here the first of the three remaining layers within the earth, which were formed, as were the outer planets, before the sun and earth separated in Hyperborea. Now that the latter are reunited, we may expect these too to be reabsorbed. The Earth Mirror (Earth Refractor) changes all characteristics into their opposites—red into green, sorrow into joy, passive into active, and vice versa. This is the sub-physical astral world, where everything moral in human nature is inverted, so that there is nothing of the good. All the forces of nature, however, such as magnetism, electricity, light or heat are transposed to spiritual or moral qualities. 'Every island vanished, there was not a mountain to be seen' (Rev. 16: 20). This layer can be perceived at the stage of 'Resurrection' or 'Divine Bliss', and in the course of moral evolution will be completely transformed.

The redeeming planet is the red Mars, whose forces represent the Old Moon evolution, when the Dynamis (Spirits of Movement) gave their astral substance for the progress of evolution. But as Spirits of Hindrance they also caused the luciferic Angels to rebel against the sun beings and form a separate moon. Though not themselves evil, they thus stand behind all luciferic evils. But through Mars they are the source of moral impulses that spring from individual character and fundamental disposition, and thus have the karma and the power to redeem those evils.

Moreover, as people absorb the wisdom that begets insight into what Christ truly is, this knowledge redeems not only themselves but also the luciferic beings—they are cleansed and purified in the fire of Christianity. The 'Holy Spirit' is none other than the unholy luciferic spirit of independent understanding (who once fell from heaven), wisdom-interwoven and resurrected in higher, purer glory. Lucifer is the bearer of light, Christ is the light.[6]

'One like a son of man' then appears with a sharp sickle to reap the harvest ... for the earth's crop is dried ... and the angel gathered the vine of the earth and cast it into the winepress of the wrath of God which flowed with blood' (Rev. 14: 14–20). There is a *pralaya* between the astral stage and that which follows.

The Intellectual Stage

In Lower Spiritland everything takes the form of thoughts, as dense as those that originally formed the brain. One either lays such thoughts into one's own being, or sends them out into the surroundings as deeds. Thoughts of the mineral creation are reabsorbed into the spirit through the regions described on page 94, but now purified and transformed by all that has since taken place. Intuition no longer sees the movements of the planets but hears clairaudiently the music of the spheres, and grasps the deeds of the different ranks of the Hierarchies.

There are still materialists who are slaves to their animal instincts and continue to oppose Christ with intelligent and malevolent opposition energetically exercised. They can neither continue in dense matter, which no longer exists, nor unite with the sun, having thrust away the sun forces. It is they who worship the beast that arises from the (sub-astral) sea with the form, power and authority of the dragon, mouthing bombast and blasphemy, which the whole world went after in wondering admiration (Rev. 13: 1–10). Such people are actually possessed by Ahriman, whose kingdom is the Counter-Lower Spiritland.

In the Divisive Layer (the Shatterer) everything evil is prepared and organized. All living forms and artistic creations (but not the shapeless inorganic) appear multiplied indefinitely, and everything strives against the other, radiating strife and disharmony to the surface. The physical human form is multiplied many times and dispersed. This layer disrupts especially the moral qualities, transforming love and compassion to harshness and brutality. The home of everything unharmonious, immoral and unpeaceful, it is responsible for evil entering the world. Dante called it the Cain layer, for the impulse to kill that is transformed into knowledge has its source here. This layer is beyond the reach of present initiation, but it is transformed by the moral development of mankind working together in harmony, in deeds—that is why it was laid down. When concord reigns it is conquered, then it works on attitudes of mind.

The counterbalance is Jupiter, whose forces represent the Old Sun, where the Kyriotetes (Spirits of Wisdom) bestowed their etheric substance, which brings inclinations and sympathies towards unity and harmony. But it is also where Ahriman was adversely commanded to his future role.

'Then war broke out in heaven. Michael and his angels waged war upon the dragon ... the great dragon was thrown down ... whose name is Satan or the devil—thrown down to earth, and his angels with him' (Rev. 12: 7). Satan, 'the unlawful prince of this world' is an exalted ahrimanic power with the rank of an Archon (Spirit of Personality), who not only aims to throw human evolution off course, but even to throw the whole earth out of orbit. He is, however, overcome by the Archangel Michael,[7] ruler of the cosmic intelligence, now himself an Archon.

The Archetypal Stage

All that now remains is raised to Higher Spiritland, where everything is again in formless, seedlike condition. This realm comprises the creative forces and purposes of the archetypes of Spirit Self, Life Spirit and Spirit Man, which have the density of the highest thoughts, such as moral ideals. The mineral condition of life is here imaged in the fixed stars, the so-called crystal sphere, where the mineral condition originated and is now reabsorbed in the realm of duration. It is in a state of absolute mobility and absolute self-control, able to shape everything out of itself. The whole human 'I' now lies naked before the world.

Through Intuition the deeds of individual beings from the ranks of the Hierarchies can be grasped. 'I heard the roar of a vast throng in heaven' (Rev. 19: 1) 'for the wedding of the Lamb has come' (Rev. 19: 7).

Progressive human beings are indeed sun beings, and Christ, who has been the Earth Spirit, is once again the Spirit of the Sun, the Sun Genius. But there is also a Sun Demon opposing the Sun Spirit, which originated from other worlds and cannot receive anything from Earth evolution. It works in the evil forces of those who have thrust away the sun and remain bound to the astral relic of the earth. 'And I saw another beast which came up out of the earth; it had two horns like a lamb's, but spoke like a dragon ... It deluded the inhabitants ... No one was allowed to buy or sell unless he bore the mark of the beast ... Its number represents the number of man, and the value of its letters is 666' (Rev. 13: 11–18). It is also known as Sorath, who seduces especially those who abuse spiritual forces in the practice of black magic (such as the deliberate cutting into flesh for the express enjoyment of the pain caused). This beast, which has a fearful power, clings to its adherents, prevents them from rising to the sun, and draws them down into the Abyss.[8]

This demon rising from the earth relates to the earth core, which immediately surrounds the centre of the earth. Forces there connect in the periphery with the human heart and brain, deeper ones with the function of the brain, and deeper ones still with propagation. Evil works there with special power, such that black magic (founded on egoism) and spiritual evil arise. Its essence, its inherent force, is separation, discord, hate, and the opposite of everything good and worthy.

The corresponding planet is Saturn, domicile of the Thrones, and representative of Old Saturn, where the Archai gained their ego. But the Asuras, Archai who have not progressed since then, not only blind people to the spirit and teach that moral ideals are mere sublimations of animal impulses, but also induce people to live like animals, with animal impulses and passions. They tear fragments out of the 'I' which are irretrievably lost, with evil consequences that cannot be expunged in the course of karma.[9] Their realm is the Counter-Higher Spiritland.

But the earth core is also the seat of Christ as Planetary Spirit. The establishing of brotherhood diminishes the evil power. Love, which spiritualizes the very body of the earth, transforms it; and black magicians will be expelled until no evil remains on earth.

The Apocalypse brings a mighty picture of this (Rev. 19: 11–16). Heaven opens to reveal descending a figure on a white horse, followed by the armies of heaven. He brings healing and justice, and makes faith and knowledge true. On his thigh (in his will) he bears the words 'King of Kings and Lord of Lords' — the name of the Lamb. And his garment, drenched in blood, is named the Word of God. His own name, like the human 'I', is known to none but himself. This figure represents the One God, but thereby also Christ himself in three guises. The light streaming from his understanding gives us an insight into Christ within ourselves at the end of this stage of evolution.[10]

Finally, apart from the Hierarchies, only progressive humanity is present, refined and concentrated in a single point like a seed in germinal condition, which contains as force everything so far experienced that is to be carried over to a new Condition of Life.

8
Conditions of Life

Introduction

With the completion of the seventh stage of form, the so-called mineral Condition of Life was also completed. This was the fourth, central condition of seven, and it will be helpful to review briefly the previous ones before going on to consider those which are to follow.

Between each Condition of Life (for example, between the 'mineral' just completed and the next, the 'plant' condition) there is a *pralaya* larger than those between stages of form, consisting of three steps, which the initiate can grasp by Intuition. It is a period of outward rest, and withdrawal into higher spheres for concentrated and intense spiritual activity. The first level is known as that of Providence or Archetypal Images, the source of the archetypal germs which give rise to Higher Spiritland. The second is a yet higher realm known as that of the Holy Spirit, which consists not so much of original creations as of combining existing processes on a new level to form a new whole, into which comes a fresh impulse from the next higher realm still, that of the Son. This then works down through the realm of Providence into manifestation.

A stage of form was in early Christian esotericism called a glory of splendour, and in theosophical usage a globe. A Condition of Life was in Christian esotericism called a kingdom, and in theosophical usage a round. And a planetary condition of consciousness was in Christian esotericism called a power. Thus in the epilogue to the Lord's Prayer, 'Thine is the kingdom, the power and the glory', the whole of evolution is ascribed to the Godhead.

The first three Conditions of Life which preceded our 'mineral' condition are recapitulated in the three elementary kingdoms which underlie the visible world of nature around us, and this can help us to understand what a Condition of Life is.

The first elementary kingdom and first Condition of Life comprise thought-seeds or intentions that become physical points of force before any form has arisen, archetypes of all that is shapeless. The elements of nature—fire, air, fluid, earth—belong here; and the physical human body, which disintegrates to dust after death, is prepared to receive its future form. Such work on the physical body alone is a recapitulation of Saturn evolution, thrice modified.

In the second Condition of Life the second elementary kingdom emerges from the first. The earth is then a very beautifully formed sphere containing the various forces woven by the world-ether thoughts, everything conceived as 'types' in the sense of Goetheanism. This includes the craftsmen of plant growth well known to earlier cultures under names such as gnomes, undines, sylphs and salamanders, and also the beings that bring about crystallization. The human etheric body and the germ of the glandular system are prepared here. This repeats the Sun evolution twice modified.

In the third Condition of Life the third elementary kingdom emerges from the foregoing. It is composed of fleeting sensations, feelings and impulses, soul-beings flying hither and thither in interpenetrating lines that express beautiful forms shining from within. A thought is a coloured cloud vibrating in itself, tones resound according to measure, number and shape. The human astral body and the germ of the nervous system are here prepared for their future task, the former appearing as a cloud of sensations not bound to any form. This is a modified repetition of the Moon evolution.

Only in our fourth (mineral) Condition of Life does there appear the world of nature all around us, which is grasped by our inorganic, mineral thinking and gives form to separate objects and our separate ego. The actual mineral kingdom is condensed out of the qualities of form of the third elementary kingdom; the plants reflect and develop out of themselves the forms of the second elementary kingdom; and the animal kingdom reflects the intentions which lie in the first elementary kingdom.[1]

The *pralaya* between the fourth and fifth conditions seems to be represented in the Apocalypse by the chaining for a thousand years of 'that serpent of old, the Devil or Satan' (Rev. 20: 2). A distinction is made between 'those who had not worshipped the beast nor received his mark', who reign with Christ for the thousand years of the *pralaya*, and 'the rest of the dead', who come to life again when the period is over in 'the first resurrection' (Rev. 20: 4) in the plant condition of life.

The Plant Condition of Life

The fifth Condition of Life of the earth that follows after the longer *pralaya* just described may be seen as a precursor of Jupiter evolution, without human beings having yet acquired the full angelic consciousness that can then be theirs. In its first stage of form the small copy of physical evolution brought over from our mineral condition reappears out of the ego in Higher Spiritland as pure memory substance. Then it is imprinted as thought substance into the ether-earth of Lower Spiritland. Thirdly, it densifies to astral light in the astral earth, and the human aura shines out. And in the fourth stage it multiplies into innumerable identical atoms which appear again in the physical. Each of these contains the whole plan of the Masters from the mineral condition of life. But there is now no actual mineral, and accordingly no solidity and no gravity. Mankind has risen half a stage higher, and everything else with it.

Human beings no longer dwell within a body, but have it outside them. They know the plant forces, such as what makes a plant grow tall, and can create and shape a new plant kingdom out of the ego. They pass through consciously the whole process which the plant today passes through unconsciously, and build their bodies out of the living substances around them. Glands secrete plantlike substances, so that if people were to spit they would spit out flowers. They no longer need to retain a hand, but can form one like a tendril when needed—everything is plantlike. They also develop higher senses with which to establish their relation to the plant world.

Everything which we today work into the mineral kingdom now reappears in all its forms as a plant kingdom. Buildings and machines are deliberately grown from the living ground—Cologne Cathedral grows as a plant, everything painted today becomes living cloud formations. The creative power present in thought pours into forming imaginations wholly permeated with life; the words which bear and sustain the images are alive. Life itself becomes objective. Plant forms and still higher things are created in the laboratory without resorting to seeds or unfamiliar forces of nature, but this is only possible when the laboratory bench is an altar, and the mixing of substances is a sacramental act.

The whole world thus becomes one single, immense living being, which may be seen as a return to the Garden of Eden at a higher level. Pupils of the Grail were told of this condition. Possessed of clear, alert consciousness, one's being was to be as pure and chaste as the calyx that turns towards the rays of the sun, the love lance; and the organs of reproduction, no longer filled with desire, were to bring forth as chastely as today the word is brought forth in the larynx. For the germ of the power of all generation, cleansed of all sexuality, is the Word.

This plant kingdom has such a supple astral body that it is formative like a law of nature, and all feelings are expressed in the form. Hence the consequences of any desire are visible, and human beings again bear in their countenance their inner qualities. The 16-petal lotus flower in the larynx now has real petals at the physical (but not mineral) stage, real vegetative leaves.

Because during our mineral condition wisdom was completely transformed into love, the astral body can now reach its highest development. At the start of this period the Dweller on the Threshold, the dragon or retarding elemental entity to whom belongs any unredeemed dross of the physical, must be killed. 'The beast [p. 94] and the false prophet [p. 99] were thrown into the lake of fire' (Rev. 19: 20). As the astral body becomes more beautiful, perceptions and feelings are perfected, and for the first time one becomes fully human in the astral body.

The majority have already put their karma in order; people can see spiritually backwards and forwards, know what karma they bring with them, and overcome it. Love exists as a reality, so that Life Spirit can to a degree come to expression.

But there are still evil ones, 'Satan will be let loose' (Rev. 20: 7); and the Manichaeans have educated others to become their teachers, who unite with the fallen ones in another attempt to bring salvation, which even black magicians can still find. Finally, 'The Devil their seducer is flung into the lake of fire and sulphur' (Rev. 20: 10). Before the end of this plant condition the decision is taken as to what is to be severed from evolution, though this is not yet carried out.

During the latter part of the period mankind draws back into itself and redeems the whole of the plant kingdom.

The Animal Condition of Life

In this sixth Life Condition, which may be seen as a precursor of Venus evolution, there is no longer any mineral or plant kingdom. 'Earth and heaven have vanished' (Rev. 20: 11). Humanity now comes to exist as a fine substance of warmth and air expressed in vibrations, sound, rhythmic or unrhythmic will, and is thus revealed to all. Breathing is fully developed, and everything taken in as light and warmth fashions the spiritual body and becomes wisdom. Human beings reproduce by uttering their likeness, and the whole atmosphere resounds with the power of the Word. Thus is fulfulled 'Let us create men in our own image' (Gen. 1: 26).

When the human heart becomes creative, one's feelings are such that through one's spirit-power one can create, as pure mental formations, sensitive beings filled with feelings and perception. Everything that streams out has within it both life and sensation. The word is an Imagination wholly filled with life, which can lead a real existence comparable to that of an animal (though unlike those of today), a bird that one sends out into the world.

Sensations and other contents of consciousness thus become objective items of knowledge, so that one can understand the feelings of another, or of an animal. Human beings thereby gain power over animal life, and at the end of this condition they are able to take into themselves and redeem the animal kingdom.

The word flows through the world as resounding being in outer corporality. That is the mystery of the Word becoming man. The divine Self is immediately present in the substance of Spirit Self.[2] Life Spirit has then to permeate the human vehicles, as Spirit Self did in the fourth Condition. Through Christian initiation one has to become what Christ has already set forth as an example. Human beings become planetary spirits, engaged with other spirits in creative work on aspects of planetary evolution. Finally the chosen of Christ, the white magicians, prepare what they possess on earth for Jupiter, sketching the outlines for the New Jerusalem.

In the fourth age of the fifth epoch (corresponding to the time of Christ's descent in our fourth Life Condition) 'the cosmic clock stands still'[3] or, one might say, those who have rejected Christ have run out of time. Everything appears desolate, for the black magicians have not just remained behind; they have developed spiritual capacities and in full consciousness placed their forces in the service of egoism, struggling stubbornly against such help. Nothing but evil then appears, with devastating power — their tendencies to evil are developed to a frightful form. The very strongest forces are now required to spiritualize those still backward, and the deepest initiates are invoked.

Now at the end of the sixth epoch of the sixth stage of form of this sixth Condition of Life comes the crucial division between everything that has been able to develop spiritually and everything else that must remain in an animal condition. *The Last Judgment* takes place (Rev. 20: 12), the great separation between good and evil that is decisive for Jupiter. Evil is overcome and hurled into the Abyss: 'Death and Hades are thrown into the lake of fire, the second death' (Rev. 20: 14). Henceforth Sorath gives to the black magicians and those who finally cut themselves off through egoism a home in the 'eighth sphere', which goes to the left and away.

The Human Condition of Life

This last Condition, the fastest of the seven, in which only progressive human beings take part, may be seen as a precursor of Vulcan evolution. Here one can form the human being anew in free activity. The goal of the earth is to pervade our whole being consciously with those vitalizing, strengthening, creative forces that are today unconsciously present during the first three years of childhood, the best forces within us. They were also present, but consciously, within Jesus from the Baptism to the Mystery of Golgotha, and through them the Son of God becomes victorious over the outcome of heredity, the Son of Man.[4]

As Imaginative consciousness is being perfected as far as possible on earth, thought is raised to an ever higher, more delicate and perfect condition. The laws governing events today regarded as chance — and much of destiny is rooted in them — come to be seen through. Indeed Christ, who brought from outside the earth that which continues to live beyond the earth, assigned to such laws the same necessity as to the laws of nature. Whilst all individual karmic debts have to be paid to the last farthing, their effects on other beings would prevent the earth from developing to Jupiter were it not that, so long as he is taken in by souls, he 'takes away the sins of the world' (John 1: 29).[5]

When various people all adopt and live with a definite common ideal, they enable a higher common consciousness to express itself through them. And when human comprehension finally embraces the wisdom of the earth, the spiritual body is completely fashioned. Only such bodies are a fit expression for him who already manifested such power in a human body. Warmth, light, everything becomes human wisdom. 'There shall be an end to death and to mourning and crying, for the old order has passed away' (Rev. 21: 4).

Everything is now present as reflected image in the ego. To dissolve one's 'I' into such a universal consciousness would however be weakness. One must above all strive for the strength to make it more and more inward and divine – the final goal can only be the community of every free and independent 'I'. Being, life and consciousness all become objective, so that the 'I' enters completely into objectivity. What results from the incarnations is finally compressed together into one dense spiritual body which Christ takes over to Jupiter to 'rise again in the body' (1 Cor. 15). All separateness is given up, and every 'I' flows together into a comprehensive consciousness – we may picture circles expanded from within, each having a separate colour, all assembled together to form one single colour.

Everyone present thus reaches the stage attained today by the Masters, concentrated in the Lodge of the Masters, where the higher self draws itself together. All seek to become similar to Christ, and gather around him like a multitude around the Lamb. In the ultimate, all human souls who follow Him are permeated by him and form a totality. That is the one reality when the earth has reached its goal.[6] Only what one has spoken in words will outlast the earth and pass into Jupiter, for it really comes from within, and through it speaks the divine Being, the Logos. The human kingdom is thus redeemed through its own strength, entirely purified and spiritualized.

Thus the earth attains its mission as the Planet of Love. The New Jerusalem, seen at this stage 'like a bride adorned for her husband' (Rev. 21: 2), arises as the fruit of this Condition, which represents the crowning of the earth.

Mankind as a whole can then become a planetary spirit, an Angel of Rotation of Time, whose body is the whole astral substance of the earth, and who has the power to drive the earth round the sun. Humanity itself becomes a god; not the highest God, but what is called a Logos of

Form. Since human beings express themselves in seven types, seven such centres actually arise, and these will become the seven Spirits of Form or Elohim of Jupiter. Mankind and Elohim are in fact but forms of one Being— that is the mystery of man becoming God.[7] The true spiritual archetypes will be infinitely scaled down, multiplied, and used as 'spiritual atoms' or building-stones for Jupiter. This entire permeation by spirit is called 'the last crisis' or more popularly 'the resurrection of the flesh'.

This final condition belongs already to Jupiter, and shines over into it.

Meditation

A star above the head
Christ speaks from the star:

Let your soul be borne
By my strong power.
   I am by you
   I am in you
   I am for you
   I am your I.

Peace of soul.

Rudolf Steiner
tr. V. Sease

Compare pages 29; 49; 50; 61–2; 87.

9

Conditions of Consciousness

Planetary Evolution

The evolution of the Earth through the stages of Saturn, Sun and Moon—part of a more extended process in which spiritual beings at many levels develop successively higher levels of consciousness—was outlined in Chapter 1, page 9. This has been a process of successive condensation, the Saturn evolution taking place on a scale comparable to the orbit of the present Saturn, the Sun to that of Jupiter today, and the Moon to that of Mars. The time has now come in which this process must be reversed on the path of re-spiritualization.

The universal principle of recapitulation before the introduction of a new element means that whereas Saturn evolution evolved in seven Conditions of Life (of which the earlier point to something unattainable even by initiate-consciousness), Sun evolution first recapitulated Saturn before developing in five Life Conditions and then re-spiritualizing; Moon recapitulated both Saturn and Sun before developing in three Life Conditions and re-spiritualizing in two stages; and the Earth evolution recapitulated all three before developing in a single Life Condition, the mineral, and respiritualizing in the three Conditions as just described.

The work of the Archai on Saturn gave rise to a very low degree of consciousness in our warmth bodies comparable to that of trance, but reaching throughout the Saturn sphere (within the orbit of its rotation). The work of the Archangels on the Sun gave rise to a one-dimensional consciousness comparable to deep sleep that extended to all that lives in light and air, like the plant's reaction to sunlight today, and formed the seed of our reflex nervous system. The work of the Angels on the Moon similarly gave rise to a living two-dimensional picture-consciousness similar to dreams, somewhat as the animals have today, which formed the basis of our hind-brain. And it is our own work on earth that gives rise to our normal waking three-dimensional consciousness based on the fore-brain, through which we rise to experience the 'I'.

Not all the beings belonging to the ranks of Archai, Archangeloi and Angeloi achieved their goal of ego-consciousness at the appropriate time, and this has given rise to a whole range of spiritual beings at intermediate stages. The hosts known as luciferic beings are Angels who remained behind on the Moon; the ahrimanic beings are Archangels who remained behind on the Sun; and those called Asuras in later lectures are Archai who remained behind on Saturn (in early lectures to theosophists all Archai were known as Asuras). Through remaining behind, their forces work out of due time, and therefore usually in an adverse way. Certain beings however renounced advancement as a sacrifice, in order to serve a special need of other beings — for example, the Spirits of Language are Spirits of Form who remained to work as Archangels for the sake of mankind.

During future embodiments of the earth it will be our task to perfect the higher states of consciousness known as Imagination, Inspiration and Intuition, the initial stages of which, as previously mentioned, can already be experienced on earth, especially by means of initiation.

Between each planetary evolution, such as between Earth and Jupiter, there is a *pralaya* which ascends through the realms of Providence and of the Holy Spirit to that of the Son, before again 'descending from heaven' (Rev. 21: 2). Outwardly it looks like a mist or fog, in which spiritual beings are continually at work. The outer turns inward, so that all the forces drawn from the earth are within us like a seed. Thus there are five stages of this *pralaya* 'on the other side of consciousness', with seven (from coma to Intuition) in manifestation, making twelve in all. The creation of a new evolution such as Jupiter requires a fresh impulse from the realm of the Father.

The new content is created out of nothingness, on the basis of the experience that went before. But it would be an intellectual error to think that the impulse for this is given during the *pralaya*. The impulse for the whole of Jupiter evolution was brought by Christ from the Father at the time of the Mystery of Golgotha, the lowest point of Earth evolution. It grows to its greatest intensity in the *pralaya*, and then during Jupiter is incorporated by a sacrifice of will by the Hierarchy that stands where the Spirits of Form stood on Earth, namely, the Spirits of Personality or Archai. The Spirits of Form guide humanity from one planetary evolution to the next. This is a level of high creative consciousness above that of Intuition, and hence beyond present human understanding. The process is similar for Venus and Vulcan.

Jupiter – The Environment

The first four Conditions of Life on Jupiter recapitulate Saturn, Sun, Moon and Earth. The latter (mineral) condition does not become solid, but only a congealed, rigidified fluid. Only during the fifth (plant) condition does the physical stage of form of Jupiter appear which is described below, 'the holy city of Jerusalem coming down out of heaven from God' (Rev. 21: 10). It takes place more quickly than does the Earth.

Only what on Earth lives enclosed by the human skin

lives over into Jupiter. In forming our body we build a temple; in doing so rightly we form Jupiter rightly. Imagine all our bodies united into a single planet—that becomes Jupiter. The inner plastic forces that today hold our physical body together then form a mineral-plant kingdom, a living mineral realm with living chemical processes, such that plant life and mineral shape are one.[1]

The Jupiter zodiac is formed by elemental beings who, unbeknown to us, work today on our twelve senses; and behind the Jupiter sun stand the elemental beings who today work into our blood system.

In our souls today we have the germ of the forms of Jupiter and all its forces. Those who study natural science form the atoms into a mineral-like sphere in the Saturn-man within us, where all our knowledge today, dead as stone, passes over in fine delicate grains into the elemental world.[2] The Archai, who were human on Saturn, today intuit what this Saturn man does in trance in our heads, and now that they rise to Spirits of Form all this becomes the forms of mineral nature. This foundation is sure and certain.[3] The gnomes preserve what is good in the firm earthly context, and incorporate it as a kind of bony support. Ideas that lead through forms of beauty, such as good music, create good beings—and the opposite. Different strata are thus formed of our thoughts and feelings, so that a Jupiter geologist might find a twentieth-century stratum formed by materialists and racketeers. Our speech too gives form to the rocklike structure, so that terrible speech gives rise to terrible structures—hence the exercise for Control of Speech.

If plants are to grow, we must acquire the ideas of spiritual science, which are active and grasped in a living way. We transform these in our Sun-man into inspirations which later densify. Without anthroposophy such ideas would float above the ground, leaving below a dead slag, so one must learn to love inner work with the ideas of anthroposophy. Archangels, now Archai, can bring the harmony of the spheres into such a definite plant growth.

Out of the picture-world of our weaving thoughts (which is the true form of our etheric body) come the forces for a plant-animal kingdom that has cosmic sensations of the processes surrounding Jupiter, and weaves around it a kind of living etheric activity. What is achieved today as art, even the substance of the Raphael *Sistine Madonna*, will arise in crystal clarity. Even our sense-perceptions, which are of a will-nature, are imprinted on the etheric body, and after death take on a coloured picture-existence which now becomes plant-animal.[4]

From that which will follow anthroposophy (p. 44), demanding of us even more inner activity, will be developed animal life. This is taken up by the Moon-man dreaming within us, and carried over by the Angels as densified Imaginations. Working then as Archangels, they establish out of it an animal kingdom.

Out of the feelings of humanity today come the conditions and character of the fluid element, and also the inner warmth. Most importantly, the love which we ourselves as individuals place into our environment on earth now comes towards us from everything around us; we perceive it and edify ourselves with it. *All beings around us pour out a fragrant, blissful love*; different grades of love emit different perfumes and tastes, as plants today emit various aromas.[5]

Jupiter – Animal-humans

Human beings on Jupiter are no longer a mixture of good and evil, but are divided into one or the other – depending on whether on earth they received the forces of Christ or stubbornly rejected them. The human astral body today contains animal impulses, and unless these are transformed they inevitably become the seed for an animal-human kingdom, which can act intelligently, but in a more automatic way than does humanity today. Such people express their karma in their form and physiognomy, which show outwardly what they are in their astral and mental bodies. If someone is a regular scoundrel, or has only animal instincts, that is what he looks like; if black magic is practised, this is known. Those who cling to the material today take on ahrimanic forms, whereas those always dreaming away in higher regions — including a good number of those belonging to spiritually minded groupings — are preparing luciferic forms.[6] Good and evil are thus outwardly visible; a great separation takes place. On Jupiter the good are surrounded by evil beings much more hostile and terrible, and in much greater numbers, than today. But one who keeps his sheaths pure and stands fast has nothing to fear.

Jupiter beings are again separated from the sun. Lucifer brings over the dead content of scattered earth-relics that have not united with Christ, but this does not now separate outside like a moon — it remains within Jupiter, constantly thrusting up. This satellite is composed of those excluded from life in the spiritual world, who suffered the 'second death' (p. 89), and have attained only an earthly 'I'-consciousness. But only earth has the ground, air, clouds, plants, minerals that this consciousness requires; on the satellite, which is quite differently fashioned, they cannot lead a normal life, but are backward beings. The luciferic souls, merely spiritual, have to experience what it means in reality to be perfected only in the ego, instead of making the whole earth one's concern. They have their bodies below, but are able to direct them only from outside, animating them like a group-soul.[7]

Those who on earth remained backward breathe air filled with stifling heat and repulsive smells, for they infect the atmosphere from the swamps, and are a cross to others.

Their bodies consist of half-solid, half-liquid substance that constantly congeals, arresting the bodily processes; they are slimy, far more repulsive than snails, exuding a crust softer than snakeskin, a kind of scaly harness. They therefore lead a very unattractive life. Whenever today we tell lies they give rise to such conditions, and even children should be taught this.[8]

The horrors committed today rise as poisonous growths; what was sown during the World War arises as poisonous marshy substance. And those who on earth have taken the '16 false paths' (p. 89) furnish a whole number of new nature-spirits with moral responsibility, who in the second half of Jupiter can no longer find bodies suitable to incarnate. The hideous forms of retarded beings with egoistic demands for love appear then as mighty devastating powers, destructive nature-powers.

All souls on Jupiter have a brief recollection of life on earth (p. 122), but those who have rejected Christ can remember nothing that happened through him. It is therefore a dreadful day of judgment for them when he does not take them with him to foster them in the second half of Jupiter, but points them away with one hand to where Ahriman takes their bodies to his treasure-house with the remains of physical matter and, with the other, points to where Lucifer leads souls on his path (where they are perfectly able to live, but unable to maintain their bodies). But there will still be a last possibility, through the strong powers of advanced beings, for even the black magicians to be saved.

Jupiter – New Humanity

As Adam was born of earth, so newly-human beings are born of Jupiter. Their sheaths are already being prepared today in the water, etheric and astral nature of our breath, which is highly differentiated (p. 52). For our earthly morality is a creative power, and in the astral texture of the breath that becomes moist our moral or immoral being is revealed. The first shadow-images must be transformed again and again by means of our pineal gland, and the further development beyond anthroposophy provides the most highly evolved concepts that make it possible for us to bring this about.

In the forms arising today from moral actions, from love, is the predisposition for the reception of an ego, and for regular progressive existence. Immoral action instead imprints on the breath demonic forms without the basis for developing an ego, and consequently condemns these beings to the hosts of Lucifer as parasites.[9] What we lay into our will today thus becomes the individual Jupiter-beings who indwell the forms that we develop.

Jupiter – Progressive Mankind

Normally progressing human beings now develop Imaginative consciousness, the dreamy Moon consciousness fully awoken, in much the same way that today earthly consciousness develops during childhood.[10] This consciousness should not be imagined within the body, but as directing the movements of the physical and etheric bodies from outside. There are of course no sense-organs such as eyes or ears, and hence no awareness of mineral substance. The physical sense-organs of today are instead transformed into inner organs. It is possible to perceive plants, and to produce complex plants in the way we today make a clock out of minerals. Into such perceptions is organized what is perceived with today's higher senses.

It is our feelings of today that blossom forth into such Imaginations, not our thoughts. The soul sketches from its external impressions with inner free will, and then makes of this the finished pictures. Parts of the soul world, especially the pains and pleasures of others, are perceptible—indeed the pictures of pain and suffering are so tormenting that one cannot feel happy until they are removed. The spiritual forms of the desires, instincts and thoughts of others appear as auras that glow and sparkle like delicate flames or clouds of light. Their colours, which arise through one's own power, are no mere images, but change into physical forms in space—the thought of a colour is colour, and so on. One can also perceive beings more delicate and spiritual, who reveal themselves in the delicate spiritual colours created from our soul; and one can influence such a being through one's image-conceptions, though the being must use its own forces to put one's desires into effect. This gradually extends to the whole astral world, so that by the end of Jupiter the level of a present Angel is attained in freedom.

It is what we create in the world today, what we make of the mineral world in architecture, painting, what we do, that constitutes our being now. The 'I' is experienced as orbiting the sphere of the sun, looking down to the earth below, surrounded by the mighty images of its thoughts and feelings shining forth like individual clouds or constellations. As today we assimilate the forces of death in order to awaken the consciousness soul, so now the forces of evil are assimilated to awaken the Spirit Self.

Our memory is quite different. Instead of looking back in time, events appear as pictures alongside one another as if congealed in space—it may be called a 'fourth dimension'. We have to move from one event to another; that is 'reading in the Akashic Record'. Inner certainty is needed to prevent mistakes, then faithfulness and exactitude increase enormously.[11] We are not only conscious of the workings of karma, but conscious in karma itself in our form and physiognomy, so that good and evil are readily recognized.

Our thoughts engender the expression of our face, which is quite soft and flexible—we go about in the guise of our enduring thoughts and temperament.

Moreover the brain and heart are completely transformed and differently placed in the body below. One is no longer a mere brain thinker, which involves moving the etheric brain whilst the physical brain is held fast. Instead the physical hands of today are enclosed in a sheath indicated by our shoulder-blades and one moves the etheric and astral hands to some extent like wings, so that what is today soul-gesture moves etherically as a new thought organ.[12] This leads to a much more living, all-embracing heart thinking, and to knowledge of the fundamental laws governing the interconnections of destiny. A 'large brain' is formed of our deeds and being today, and our thoughts form a 'small brain' that warns like a judge. Wrong thoughts again cause an instant change of expression.

The spiritualized heart is formed no longer from the world of spirit but from the higher instreaming world of Archetypal Images, which stands above the world of Reason; and it beholds the truth out of direct feeling.[13] The ego directs the blood inwards to strengthen itself, so it can overcome evil without anxiety; or drives it to the periphery to achieve harmony with the world and enable its inmost force to stream outwards.

We no longer breathe in air from outside, but have an organ to work it over within us as we do today with warmth. Instead we breathe in light and live in light. The physical body is no longer subject to gravity—having mastered physical substance we are subject to moon forces which draw us away from the earth, so we can move up steep slopes like a fly.

It is of the very nature of spiritual knowledge to become love. As today we evolve wisdom, so now we develop love, wafting love to those around us. Earth warmth, rays of

sunlight, everything we sensed on earth becomes new forces streaming out of us. And out of human work, human
love, arises peace.

There can of course be no question of life and death. The
soul relates to its surroundings in such a way that its existence is not interrupted against its will; it has become lord
over life and death.

In the moral quality of today we have the seed of a
common life of people grouped in large regions. All the
thoughts, feelings and experiences we today ray out after
death into the cosmos now enable us to unfold Spirit Self,
woven as an image of the earth. We relate to this as we do to
our 'I' today—it belongs to us, but we are still working on
it.[14] Meanwhile the ego begins the real work of transforming the light that shines towards the etheric body into Life
Spirit, for which the help of Christ is again needed.

In the middle of life, for a short time symbolized by 'three
days', we have a mighty inner dream vision of all we
actually achieved during Earth evolution, as real as is perception today. With our body we no longer fit our surroundings, as if at 35 we could no longer breathe, nor eat or
drink. We meet a being we know to be Lucifer, and know
that we worked through with him all that we wished to
become on earth; and we cannot do other than follow him.
Lucifer could lead away our souls, had not Christ amassed
treasures in us during the first part of our Jupiter life which
sustain us through the second half. Only through remembering Christ's appearance on earth do we know that he
brought gifts which now enable us to take instead the path
of the genuinely developing cosmos. All that has been
attempted through the indwelling of Christ forms the balance between the ahrimanic and luciferic forms. Thus
everything depends on our souls remembering how they
filled themselves with understanding that Christ had
entered Earth evolution.[15] The Christ Ego in the astral and

etheric bodies goes on to ensoul existence on Jupiter, and one who turns away from Christ deprives himself of this for the whole of future evolution.

Similarly, luciferic Angels, Archangels and Archai who on earth rejected Christ form a certain union with what as planetary residue is out in the universe. They still hanker after an influence on humanity and can descend to fleshly embodiments.

We thus receive recognizable influences from very different realms, and can act consciously on very different forces and powers from those of today. At the end of Jupiter our earthly feelings of desire finally absorb the plant kingdom. From then on, we can speak only of the evolution of the good.

Venus Evolution

The first five Conditions of Life on Venus recapitulate the previous planetary evolutions; only at the physical stage of the sixth (animal) condition do the circumstances described below appear. The realities of life then cannot be grasped by the limited reason of today. The planet remains permanently united with the sun for all time, so that all beings are actually sun-beings. But it is now at a higher stage than the sun of today, for all the beings previously cast off have been reunited. The speed and conditions of the Old Sun evolution are regained, and the wide-ranging sleep consciousness of that time is now fully awakened to Inspiration. Everything given to us up to the first half of Earth evolution has now been stripped off.

There are no mineral or plant kingdoms, the lowest being the animal; but there are three human kingdoms in different degrees of perfection. All substance, including the bodies, consist only of air and warmth. As a stag casts its antlers, so human beings dispense with what corresponds to the head in the middle of life, and grow another out of the limb forces. They have to control consciously from outside all the single molecules of their brain. The knee-cap of today gives rise to a complete skull-like enclosure that contains the organ of consciousness. And today's lower legs and feet, with what they receive from the earth, become organs leading to spiritual worlds — kneeling in prayer prepares us for this.[16]

Without our feelings of today, the forces needed for the forming of Venus would not be present. The forces of sculpture especially work then in purified form — the *Venus de Milo* is an expression of this. Our desires and wishes reappear as fully conscious Inspirations, in which the soul not only lives in images but creates objects and beings. We then rule the creative forces of other realms to the extent that we can at will produce effects by means of images, without the being affected having to use its own forces. Through the spoken word, creative feelings give rise to actual forms in the surrounding air, so that we are surrounded by creations of our own speech — if we utter an evil word, something like a repulsive organism comes into existence. Venus may thus be called the planet of the Word or Logos, because the word imparts meaning, and everything that appears stupid or illogical is cast off.

We live today amid sun forces that are hidden but active in the workings of karma, bringing together individuals as yet unknown to one another. Through these forces one can now illuminate the spiritual darkness so as to reflect back an Imagination of the world totality.[17] We only understand Christ today because he enabled disciples such as Peter or James after their death to reach such understanding in the third century through these very forces of Venus already latent, and to inspire those who wrote about the Mystery of Golgotha.

One experiences another person through their effect on one's breathing, perceiving their whole inner character of soul in the form of sound, so that they seem like a musical form within the astral picture. Social life on Venus resembles the beehive, which is built of carbon created out of its own being, has a consciousness at the Imaginative level, and where work is the main concern.

Consciousness develops in the transformed etheric body. Lower Spiritland lies fully open to it, and during sleep one is conscious of 'the other side of the world'. It is concerned with the development of Life Spirit, and comes from the realm belonging today to the Archangels, where Christ is the directing and guiding principle. For the work which begins to transform the physical warmth-air body to Spirit Man a further helper is required who is designated 'the Father'. The Father Principle, the Hidden God, who was already an adept on Saturn, can now incarnate.

Thus does our will point to Venus. It is destined eventually to absorb the animal kingdom, as the mineral is absorbed on earth.

When the sixth (intellectual) stage of form is reached during the sixth Condition of Life on Venus (the sixth planet) — 666 — then for those who have persistently rejected the forces of Christ and have still not developed beyond the 'I'-consciousness of today (if indeed there are any) comes the last, unalterable separation. A separate celestial body is detached, an 'irreclaimable moon', which includes all beings who have persisted in withstanding the true course of evolution. This no words can portray.

Nothing of what is now called matter can pass beyond Venus; only that part of the human being accessible to supersensible knowledge is the germ of something that continues.

Vulcan Evolution

It was said in the mysteries: No soul which with its thinking is still tied to a physical body should reflect about Vulcan and its life.

The first six Conditions of Life recapitulate previous evolutions; only in the seventh (human) condition does the new unfold. Mankind now exists only in Higher Spiritland, clearly beyond the reach of present thought.

The human being does not incarnate, but by means of the word builds out of his own being a body of warmth substance like a soft diamond as required. Of the present form, there remain only the two-petal lotus (which develops into two wings like the two horns of Michelangelo's Moses) and the transformed left side of the breast and left hand as an organ of movement. The heart replaces the brain as organ of consciousness, the three parts of which— thinking, feeling and willing—are completely separated. The pineal and pituitary glands organize a second spinal column descending in front, which later unites with the first. The lower part of the body and the right side, which came from the past, must disappear, to be raised later to a higher stage. Hence Vulcan was depicted in the mysteries with a limp.[18] Esoteric knowlege of today becomes physical as blood.

All the beings who evolved from the small beginnings of Saturn are now spiritualized to the highest degree, and Vulcan contains only what has been absorbed by the human kingdom. The capacity of Intuition, or 'creative spiritual consciousness', based on transformation of the will, is called upon to become both cosmic and powerful. When this consciousness leaves the physical, withdrawing also the etheric, it can acquire exact self-conscious knowledge of the whole universe and its beings. It is a full awakening of the trance-consciousness of Saturn, which reaches to the fixed stars. To the emptiness of world space, individuals present their own fullness, identifying with and living with the beings in their field of awareness, yet remaining individual. Human beings thus belong to the whole cosmos, their individual impulses are applied to cosmic deeds. One may compare the consciousness of Archai, who today reach down only to the realm of warmth. Christ was already manifesting this stage at the Mystery of Golgotha.

This consciousness lives out individual impulses which continue to exist in warmth and cold outside itself. Every deed is actualized and becomes reality in the warmth. Work is now the highest principle. We see the beginnings of this, wrapped in deep unconsciousness, in repetitive work today — when a worker makes something like nails, he does not follow up each one to see what becomes of it, but lets it take its own way in the world. By doing so he actually creates a seed of future values. But on Vulcan this is connected with the great sacrifices expressed in the words 'Thy will be done'.

At the end of Vulcan, mankind has the form of an archetype in Higher Spiritland. This is a fully purified condition of godliness or divine bliss, the highest stage accessible to humanity, into which the fruits of all planetary evolutions are gathered. Then one can truly say: 'I am the Alpha and the Omega', the whole divine world from Saturn through Golgotha. Human circumstances are now graded according to karma in seven grades of morality. As individuals transform the forces of the physical warmth body into Spirit Man, they develop stage by stage (but not in time) the capacity to work upwards towards the constellation of the Balance. Together they become not just a sun, but what was sun on Venus ascends to heavenly existence as a sun within a sun, an 'over-sun'. This is the fruit of experiences with things of physical space, such as an alternation of waking and sleeping consciousness, which those beings who have remained within the sun through previous evolutions could never have themselves achieved.

*   *   *

Subsequently mankind becomes a hollow, a choir of beings like Seraphim, Cherubim and Thrones, and advances to new creative tasks. It reaches the maturity capable of sacrifice, self-dissolution, comparable to the Spirits of Form on earth, who sacrificed their ego-substance for mankind. Something streams out from mankind in the realm of duration, eternity. It becomes a new zodiac, a creative god, and will build a planet[19] and bring forth suns. Seven of its forces are ascending, to form a new cosmic evolution; whilst five, like the constellations from Scorpio to Pisces today, rain down — the mysterious 'heavenly ladder'.

Mankind ascends to yet higher stages — the inner eye of the initiate sees five beyond Vulcan, making twelve in all, towards which the Hierarchies already lead the way; but they cannot be described in human language.

Appendices

1 *The Human Being Seen Spiritually*

A spiritual-scientific study of evolution begins with experience and understanding of our own nature, not only during life but also between death and rebirth. Rudolf Steiner presented the results of his spiritual research in this field in many places, but first in his book *Theosophy* (1904).

We need to distinguish first the three aspects of body, soul and spirit. The body as outer object is a given fact for sense-perception. The soul is experienced only within oneself, and is found to include thoughts, feelings, passions, sensations and impulses of will. The spirit is again objective, a goal of awareness of beings who manifest as truth, beauty and goodness, towards which we must continually strive. Each of these is complex, but their main features may be all too briefly summarized as follows.

The body is subject to heredity, and has three aspects:

- The physical body is a mineral structure which, when sustained by the principles outlined below, has a form perceptible to the senses and understandable by the intellect. When not so sustained, its substance dissolves into a pile of chemicals subject to inorganic laws.
- The life-body or etheric body is a supersensible entity which distinguishes the living from the dead, the plant and higher kingdoms from the mineral. It is essentially a time-organism, related to rhythms such as those of the month or year, and thereby also to cosmic influences. It manifests as formative processes such as breathing, warming, nourishing, secreting, sustaining, growing and reproduction.

- The sentient body is that inherited supersensible centre of activity which distinguishes the animal and human kingdoms from the merely vegetative, those organisms that have sensations, feelings and instincts from those which do not. It manifests essentially in a dreamy awareness of its own life-processes that in turn mirror its environment.

The human soul is subject to karma, exists in time but not in space, and likewise has three aspects:

- The sentient soul is a fountain of inner activity through which sense-processes become sensations of phenomena external to itself, and desire and aversion, impulses and passions become facts of experience leading to action. It is present in all people including primitive cultures.

  Sentient body and sentient soul frequently work as a unity known as the astral body. It is fundamentally a body of desires.
- The intellectual soul is subject to the laws of thought, transcends both immediate experience and personal limitations, and issues in intended deeds. The ego first comes to manifestation in the intellectual soul, which may be personally developed to a greater or lesser extent. It is also called the mind soul or emotional-thought soul.
- The consciousness soul or spiritual soul is that in which truth, beauty and goodness shine forth, freed from all feelings of sympathy or antipathy, and brings about premeditated deeds in freedom. It must be consciously developed by each individual.

The spirit is subject to reincarnation, existing neither in space nor time (so that past and future are equally present to it) and is also threefold:

- Spirit Self, as yet present for most people only as a seed, results from the conscious spiritual effort of the individual to master and transform the soul, especially in the realm of thinking. It develops a higher form of inner consciousness called Imagination, and forms a finely woven planetary existence reflected from the earth. It forms a unity with the consciousness soul like a sword within its scabbard.

- Life Spirit arises from the individual transformation of the etheric body, especially in the realm of feeling, and then unfolds the higher form of consciousness called Inspiration. It is already foreshadowed in compassion.
- Spirit Man* is the future transformation of the physical body, especially in the realm of deed, into a spiritual entity in harmony with the universe. It develops by means of the consciousness known as Intuition.

Because of the way in which it operates, humanity may also be understood as comprising seven parts: physical, etheric and astral bodies, ego, spirit-filled consciousness soul, Life Spirit and Spirit Man. These are referred to in the Apocalypse as the 'seven spirits of God' in man (Rev. 3: 1).

When incarnating in our age, the spirit, which belongs to the unchanging, eternal realm of the fixed stars, draws together soul-substance from the ever-changing sphere of the planets, which in turn reaches down into the body that is born of earth through heredity. During sleep the soul carries the day's events back into the planetary realm and refreshes its forces there. After death these night-experiences are worked over by the soul, and their fruits are then absorbed by the spirit to form new capacities. At all levels except the physical, beings interpenetrate and permeate one another.

---

*One should not fear to use the time-honoured word 'Man' for the sake of a political correctness arising from sexuality. 'Man' derives from 'Manas' the Spirit Self, and from 'Manu', a spiritual leader of mankind. Other Hierarchies have passed through their human stage in the past, but only human beings of the present undergo their evolution as Man.

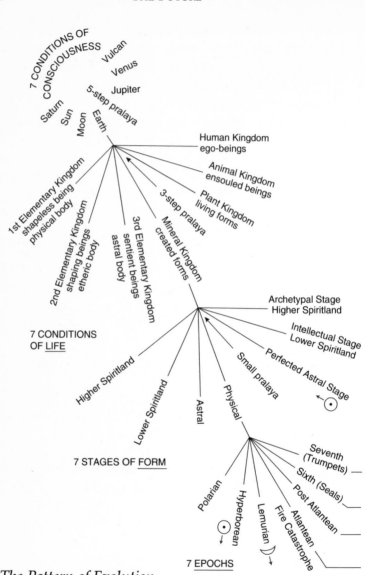

2. The Pattern of Evolution

(Rudolf Steiner says that such a scheme is 'related to the full reality not even like the inner framework of a house to the complete building, but only like the outer scaffolding ... that has to be taken down when the building is complete'.)

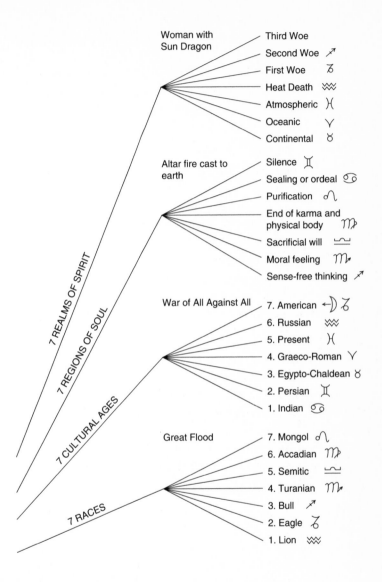

3 Concerning the Lord's Prayer
(RGS)

The path of evolution known to the mysteries is so fundamental that it also lies hidden within religious documents.
This may be indicated by the Lord's Prayer as follows:

Post-Atlantean Epoch
Fourth Age: Our Father in the Heavens
   Christ brings the new impulse from the Father that leads
   to Jupiter — p. 114
Present Age: Hallowed be thy name
   The path begins with reverence for truth and knowl-
   edge — p. 21
Sixth Age: Thy kingdom come
   The etheric world becomes visible to all — p. 48
Seventh Age: Thy will be done
   A new form of life is inevitable, with all it entails — p. 54

Sixth Epoch (Seals)
First Age: On earth as in heaven
   Creation from peripheral consciousness — p. 69
Second Age: Give us this day our supersensible* bread
   Need for spiritual strength to 'turn the other cheek' — p. 73
Third Age: Forgive us our debts
   Manichaeism transmutes evil through forgiveness — p. 75
Fourth Age: As we forgive our debtors
   Final balancing of karma — p. 76

---

*The word *epiousion* was newly coined by the Greek translator for an
Aramaic original unknown to us. Origen, almost a contemporary, said it
meant 'the divine essence for maintaining the divinity in us'. The Cathar
manuscript of Lyons translates it 'supersubstantialem'. Others detect a
hint of the future. It has no connection with *Semeron* — today.
   Bread = manna = Manas = Spirit Self.

Fifth Age: Bring us not into temptation
　　Clothing in innocence — p. 78
Sixth Age: Deliver us from the evil
　　Evil race drawn down into the Abyss — p. 81
Seventh Age: For thine is the kingdom
　　Silence in heaven, free soul outpouring — p. 82

Bibliographical References

Note: All references are to the work of Rudolf Steiner unless otherwise indicated. Published English translations are available from Rudolf Steiner Press (UK) or Anthroposophic Press (USA). The lectures listed below by date only may be traced at the Rudolf Steiner Library, 35 Park Road, London NW1 6XT, or other major anthroposophical libraries. The former also holds typescripts and original German texts.

Written volumes are identified by initials as follows:

CM	*Cosmic Memory*
CMF	*Christianity as Mystical Fact*
GW	G. Wachsmuth, *Evolution of Mankind*, Dornach CH 1961
KHW	*Knowledge of Higher Worlds*
K 1	Undated lecture, Typescript
OS	*An Outline of Occult Science*
T	*Theosophy*
VM	*Verses and Meditations*

Passim

To the zodiac:

7.6.12	*Man in the Light of Occultism*, 5
21.1.14	*Human and Cosmic Thought*, 2
22.1.14	Ibid, 3
28.10.21	*Cosmosophy*, Vol. 2, 4
7.7.24	*Eurythmy as Visible Speech*

To colour:

6.5.21	*The Nature of Colour*, 1

To the interior of the earth:
see Chapter 5, ref. 2

1 *Introduction*

1.	7.3.11	*Background to the Gospel of St Mark*, 8
2.	27.6.08	*The Apocalypse of St John*, 8
3.	17.6.08	*Apocalypse of St John*, Intro.
4.	1.11.19	*Lucifer and Ahriman*, 1
5.	7.12.13	*The Mysteries of the East and of Christianity*, 4
6.	28.7.24	*Karmic Relationships*, III, 7
7.	4.11.19	*Lucifer and Ahriman*, 3
8.	22.5.08	*The Gospel of St John*, 4
	31.12.12	*The World of the Senses and the World of the Spirit*, 5
9.	20.5.08	*The Gospel of St John*, 3
10.	26.5.08	*The Gospel of St John*, 7
11.	6.8.18	Typscript C50, 7
12.	10.10.11	*From Jesus to Christ*, 6 et seq.
13.	11.10.11	*From Jesus to Christ*, 7

Also consulted:

The Being of Christ
22.4.07, 18/30.5.08, 17.6.08, 2/3.7.09, 23.8.10, 6.6.11, 8.9.24

2 *The Future of the Fifth Age*

1.	15.11.19	*Lucifer and Ahriman*, 4
2.	6.2.17	*Cosmic and Human Metamorphoses*, 1
3.	18.11.17	*The Reappearance of Christ in the Etheric*, 10
4.	1.5.13	*Occult Science and Occult Development*, 1
5.	25.11.17	*The Reappearance of Christ in the Etheric*, 12
6.	9.2.20	Not translated. GA 266/3
7.	16.8.19	*Anthroposophical News Sheet*, 1944
8.	21.9.11	*Anthroposophical Quarterly*, Vol. 64 No. 3
9.	25.1.10	*The True Nature of the Second Coming*, 1
10.	26.10.18	*From Symptom to Reality*, 5
11.	20.10.23	*Man as Symphony of the Creative Word*, 2
12.	6.11.17	*Behind the Scenes of External Happenings*, 1

13. 20.11.14   *The World as Product of the Working of Balance*, 1
14. 7.12.18   *The Challenge of the Times*, 5
15. 13.5.21   *The Golden Blade*
16. 17.1.15   *Destinies of Individuals and of Nations*, 4
17. 19.11.17   *The Reappearance of Christ in the Etheric*, 11

Also Consulted:

The End of Michael's Rulership
31.10.06, 18.4.09, 27.2.10, 15/29.3.10, 9.9.10, 21.9.11, 7.10.11,
2.12.11, 15.7.14, 20.11.14, 6.2.20, OS, KHW, VM

Oriphiel's Rulership
16.12.04, 10.11.05, 2.1.06, 18/23.10.07, 16/26.1.08, 22.3.09, 27.2.10,
22.3.13, 7.11.16, 18.11.17, 25.6.18, 16.7.18, 1.12.18, 28.11.19, 23.3.23,
10.6.24, 8.8.24

Anael's Rulership
3.11.18, 12.12.18, 18.3.23, 30.8.23

Zachariel's Rulership
20.5.12, 16.12.17, 9.9.24

Raphael's Rulership
14.6.06, 5.6.07, 1/24/30.6.08, 5/16.8.08, 20.11.14, 13.2.15, 20.10.18,
3.1.19, 13.10.23, 15/22.8.24

Passim
22.1.14, 7.12.18, T, KB

3 The Sixth Age

1. 20.5.17   *Anthroposophical News Sheet*, 1943
    29.5.17   *Aspects of Human Evolution*, 1
2. 13.4.08   *Easter*, 6
3. 7.11.15   *Anthroposophical News Sheet*, 1940
4. 19.11.22   *Planetary Spheres*, 6
5. 5.6.07   *Theosophy of the Rosicrucians*, 7
6. 11.9.10   *The Gospel of St Matthew*, 11

7. 9.2.05   Not translated. GA 53
8. 7.3.11   *Background to the Gospel of St Mark*, 8
9. 31.5.08   *The Gospel of St John*, 11
10. 9.7.18   Typescript C 50, 3
11. 18.10.05   *Foundations of Esotericism*, 20
12. 26.10.18   *From Symptom to Reality in Modern History*, 5
13. 4.12.09   *The Ego*, 1
14. 4.11.11   *Jeshu ben Pandira*, 1
15.   Ibid.
    1.10.11   *The Reappearance of Christ in the Etheric*, 5
16.   Ibid.
17.   As ref. 13

Also consulted:

The New Conditions
4.11.05, 26.6.07, 7.3.11, 13.3.15, 15.6.15, 25.10.15, 7.11.15, 24.1.17,
12.4.17, 30.3.18, 3.11.18, 23.3.23, 9.9.24, CM xviii

The Awakening of the 'I'
30/31.10.05, 14.6.06, 15.5.07, 26.6.07, 12.8.08, 4.12.09, 28.5.10,
21.9.11, 30.5.12, 15.6.15, 27.12.18, 9.9.24

The Reception of Spirit Self
9.02.05, 30.5.08, 26/29.6.08, 22.3.09, 26.12.09, 15/29.3.10, 9.9.10,
22.8.11, 15.6.15, 20.2.17, 4.6.24

Christ and the Maitreya
3.10.05, 12.2.06, 14.6.06, 13.4.08, 20.6.08, 12.8.08, 14.5.09, 30.8.09,
25.9.09, 27.2.10, 7.3.11, 8/12.6.11, 21.8.11, 19/21.9.11, 12.3.13,
3.1.15, 12.4.17, 27.12.18, K 1

4 *The Seventh Age*

1. 18.1.20   *The Golden Blade*, 1960
2. 28.10.17   *The Fall of the Spirits of Darkness*, 6
3. 4.10.05   *Foundations of Esotericism*, 9
4. 12.4.17   *Building Stones*, 4

5. 26.10.18   *From Symptom to Reality in Modern History*, 5
6. Undated   Typescript K 1
7. 16.11.17   *Geographic Medicine*
8. 31.10.05   *Foundations of Esotericism*, 28
9. 23.3.23   *The Driving Force of Spiritual Powers in World
                History*, 7
10. 4.11.23   *Man as Symphony of the Creative Word*, 9
11. 13.5.21   *The Golden Blade* 1960
12. 23.12.04   *Temple Legend*, 10
13. 21.9.11   *Anthroposophical Quarterly*, 1964/3

Also consulted:

A Culture of Will
23.12.04, 2.10.05, 8.7.06, 6.6.07, 16.9.07, 25.5.08, 25.6.08, 11/12/
16.8.08, 2.9.08, 14/15.9.09, 21.8.11, 4.11.11, 31.12.15, 10.10.16, 20/
29.5.17, 30.8.23

The Ending of our Epoch
31.12.04, 14.6.06, 8.5.07, 25.6.08, 11.5.09, 8/10.6.10, 7.3.11, 13.9.19,
OS

Christ's Tiny Band
7.3.07, 20.6.08, 14.5.09, 9.9.10, 4/18.11.11, 3.12.11, 7.12.18

5 *The Sixth Epoch (Seals)*

1. 2.2.10   *The Christ-Impulse and the Development of Ego-
              Consciousness*, 1
2. 4.9.06   *At the Gates of Spiritual Science*, 14
              Also 16.4.06, 21.4.06, 12.6.06, 11.7.06, 1.1.09, and for future
              references to the interior of the earth
3. 17.2.23   *Cosmic Workings in Earth and Man*, 2
4. 25.6.08   *The Apocalypse of St John*, 8
5. 29.8.06   *At the Gates of Spiritual Science*, 8
6. 27.9.05   *Foundations of Esotericism*, 2
7. 5.6.05   *The Temple Legend*, 14

8. 14.5.12   *Earthly and Cosmic Man,* 6
9. 31.10.06 Not translated. GA 55
10. 19.5.09 *Reading the Pictures of the Book of Revelation,* 2/10
11. 19.3.05 Typescript Z 327

Also Consulted:

The Seven Epochs
29.10.04, 31.8.06, 15.5.07, 16.9.07, 19/25/30.6.08, 7.9.08, 18.4.09,
11.5.09, 1.1.12, 31.8.13, 13.2.15, 29.11.17, 10.1.21, OS, CM viii, T

The First Three Ages
11.11.04, 2.10.05, 13.2.06, 14.6.06, 25.10.06, 6.6.07, 21/24/30/
31.6.08, 11/17/18.5.09, 19.5.10, 7.3.14, 12/19.4.17, 7.12.18,
21.10.21, 1.7.22, 19.11.22, CMF ix, T

The Fourth Age
7.10.04, 6.10.05, 4.11.05, 21/30.6.08, 31.12.11, CMF ix, OS, T, GW

The Last Three Ages
29.5.05, 7.10.05, 3.11.05, 15.5.07, 18/21/24.6.08, 18.5.09, 1.4.13,
15.10.13, 31.12.15, 20.2.17, 21.10.21, CMF ix, OS, T

6 *The Seventh Epoch (Trumpets)*

1. 16.5.20   *Man: Hieroglyph of the Universe* (revised trans-
             lation published under the title *Mystery of the
             Universe*), 16
2. Ibid.
3. 16.7.14   *Christ and the Human Soul,* 4
4. 31.10.06 Not translated. GA 94

Also consulted:

The First Four Ages
31.10.04, 29.9.05, 19.10.05, 14.6.06, 26.1.07, 1/8.5.07, 16.9.07, 25.6.08, 20.5.09, 1.4.13, 31.8.13, 23.11.19, 21.10.21, 1.12.21, OS, T

Fifth and Sixth Ages
23.8.06, 16.9.07, 16.5.08, 25/26/30.6.08, 19.5.09, 31.10.11, CMF ix, T

The End of the Physical/Etheric Earth
5/10/21/28.10.05, 25/26/30.6.08, 12.8.08, 18.4.09, 28.5.10, 21.8.11, 7.9.24, T

7 *Stages of Form*

1.	28.10.05	*Foundations of Esotericism*, 26
2.	2.11.04	Typescript R 73
3.	26.6.08	*The Apocalypse of St John*, 9
4.	15.9.24	*The Book of Revelation*, 11
5.	18.10.15	*Occult Movements in the 19th Century*, 5
6.	22.3.09	*The Deed of Christ*, 1
7.	15.9.24	*The Book of Revelation*, 11
8.	29.6.08	*The Apocalypse of St John*, 11
9.	22.3.09	*The Deed of Christ*, 1
10.	14.9.24	*The Book of Revelation*, 10

Also consulted:

The Perfected Astral Stage
7/9/26/31.10.05, 25.11.05, 16.9.07, 25/27.6.08, 11.11.08, 19/20.5.09, 19.9.24

The Intellectual Stage
16.1.05, 20.4.08, 29.6.08, 27.3.13, 14.2.20, 22.9.24

The Archetypal Stage
25/29.10.04, 5/26.10.05, 16.9.07, 30.6.08, 1.10.11, T

8 *Conditions of Life*

1. 27.10.05   *Foundations of Esotericism*, 25
2. 17.10.04   Typescript R 73, 1
3. 31.10.06   Not Translated. GA 94
4. 25.2.11   *Anthroposophical Quarterly*, 1976/4
5. 15.7.14   *Christ and the Human Soul*, 3
6. 8.5.12   *Anthroposophical Quarterly*, Vol. 18, No. 1
7. 9.11.04   Typescript R 73, 1

Also consulted:

Introduction
29.10.04, 26/31.10.05, 10.6.06, OS iv, T

Plant Condition of Life
17/22/31.10.04, 5.11.04, 16.1.05, 13/19.3.05, 29.9.05, 5/21/26/27/28.10.05, 5.6.07, 2.12.07, 27.6.08, 20.5.09

Animal Condition of Life
25/31.10.04, 16.1.05, 4/8/26/28.10.05, 11.6.06, 5.6.07, 27/29.6.08, 20.5.09

Human Condition of Life
22/25.10.04, 8/9/27/28/29.10.05, 1/14.6.06, 24.3.08, 26.6.08, 10.10.11, 26.3.12, 8.5.12, 15.7.14, 1.12.21

9 *Conditions of Consciousness*

1. 9.10.21   *Cosmosophy*, Vol. 1, 8
2. 22.6.15   *The Destinies of Individuals and of Nations*, 11
3. 3.6.15   Typescript Z 167
4. 9.10.21   As ref. 1
5. 24.3.08   *The Influence of Spiritual Beings upon Man*, 6
6. 9.10.21   As ref. 1
7. 16.7.14   *Christ and the Human Soul*, 4
8. 6.3.11   *The Significance of Spiritual Research for Moral Action*

9. 3.1.15   Typescript Z 163
10. 3.4.15   *Festivals of the Seasons*
11. 30.3.10   *Macrocosm and Microcosm*, 10
12. 6.10.14   *Occult Reading and Occult Hearing*, 4
13. 30.3.10   As ref. 11
14. 21.10.21 *Cosmosophy*, Vol. 2, 1
15. 3.4.15   As ref. 10
16. 6.10.14   As ref. 12
17. 25.8.23   *The Evolution of Consciousness*, 7
18. 6.6.06   *An Esoteric Cosmology*, 10
19. 28.9.05   *Foundations of Esotericism*, 3

Also consulted:

Planetary Evolution
26/30.10.05, 14.6.06, 15.4.09, 30.3.10, 8.6.10, CM xiv, OS

Jupiter—The Environment
4/8/27.10.05, 26.6.08, 12.8.08, 13.4.09, 20.5.09, 26.4.14, 18.7.20, 21.10.21, 4.11.23, CM xiii, OS

Jupiter—Animal-humans
29.10.04, 16/26.1.08, 16.5.08, 30.6.08, 3.4.15, 30.8.23

Jupiter—New Humanity
4.10.05, 26.6.08, 3.6.15

Jupiter—Progressive Mankind
29.10.04, 23.12.04, 9.10.05, 9.12.05, 2.10.06, 15.9.07, 16.1.08, 27/30.6.08, 12.8.08, 20.5.09, 7.6.10, 21.8.11, 21.9.11, 14.7.14, 9.3.15, 3.4.15, 1.4.18, 26.10.18, 14.2.20, 28.3.20, 9/21.10.21, 25.8.23, CM xiii

Venus Evolution
29.10.04, 26.9.05, 25/27.10.05, 16/27.1.08, 27/29/30.6.08, 17.1.09, 5.3.09, 14.4.09, 28.10.09, 13.3.17, 5.10.18, 26.10.18, 26/27.11.20, 31.8.23, 7.9.24, CM xiii, OS

Vulcan Evolution
29.10.04, 29.9.05, 26/27.10.05, 16.9.07, 27.1.08, 27.6.08, 14.4.09, 12.6.11, 6.11.16, 14.2.20, 30.8.23, 7.9.24, CM xiii/xiv

Richard Seddon
MANI
His Life and Work
Transforming Evil

Who was Mani? Historical sources tell that he founded a successful spiritual movement across Asia, Africa and parts of Europe, which was then brutally suppressed. Many fragments of written works are still being discovered and translated, revealing aspects of his teachings. However, from his own spiritual research Rudolf Steiner gave key insights which provide an important esoteric source in helping to solve more fully the mystery surrounding Mani.

In this factual survey, invaluable for any serious student of esotericism, Richard Seddon pieces together the puzzle — from both esoteric and exoteric sources — to present a comprehensive picture of Mani. From this succinct outline of Mani's life and individuality, the fundamental aspects of his teaching, and the future role of Manichaism, a picture emerges of a mighty spiritual figure. We see Mani as a great Christian initiate directing a movement with a critical task spread over many millennia: the transformation and redemption of evil.

ISBN 0 904693 95 3; £8.95

Richard Seddon
EUROPA
A Spiritual Biography

From his spiritual research Rudolf Steiner spoke of history as more than the outcome of mere cause and effect on the physical plane. He stated that human beings are influenced, usually unconsciously, by spiritual beings — especially the Archangels of Time and the Archangels working as Folk Spirits and Language Spirits of the various peoples.

Europa, A Spiritual Biography offers a unique view of history in that it considers Europe from the point-of-view of the rulerships of the various Archangels of Time — from Michael's regency between the mid-sixth and the third century BC, up to his present rulership between 1879 and the twenty-second century. Richard Seddon gives a clear overview of Steiner's many results of research, set against an outline of outer events extended to the present day. Detailed references give the reader the possibility of studying further Steiner's own words.

ISBN 0 904693 72 4; £8.95